Taming of the Team

How Great Teams Work Together

by Jack Berckemeyer

Foreword by Dr. Debbie Silver

IncentivePublications

BY WORLD BOOK

and

Association for Middle Level Education
4151 Executive Parkway, Suite 300
Westerville, Ohio 43081 | www.amle.org

D1127653

This book is dedicated to several people who have had a direct impact on my life:

To my mother, Sharon Marie Berckemeyer, who raised and tamed me at the same time. In the play Billy Elliot, *Billy's mentor says to him, "She must have been a very special person, your mother." Billy replies, "No, she was just me mom."*

To Kathy Hunt Ullock, "Because I knew you, I have been changed for good."

To Jan Blatchford and Judith Baenen, for all their support and kindness.

To Josie Berck McCloud, my sunshine.

To William "Bill" Wheeler, Joel Showalter, and Jeff Turner, for their unconditional friendship.

To Debbie Silver, for writing the foreword to my book and making me laugh.

And a special thanks to these hardworking teams who validate the idea that taming the team leads to the best show for students, administrators, families, and teachers:

- *Central High School, the 9th Grade Center, and Block Middle School, East Chicago, Indiana*
- *Whittier and Memorial middle schools in Sioux Falls, South Dakota*
- *Stillwater Middle School, Stillwater, Oklahoma*
- *Arcola Intermediate, Methacton School District, Eagleville, Pennsylvania*
- *Lima West and Lima Magnet in Lima, Ohio*
- *Perkins Local School District—Perkins High School and Briar Middle School, Perkins, Ohio*
- *Sandusky High School and Sandusky Middle School, Sandusky, Ohio*

Illustrated by Kathleen Bullock
Cover by Debbie Weekly
Edited by Jill Norris and Marjorie Frank
Copyedited by Carla Weiland

Print Edition ISBN 978-1-62950-002-7
E-book Editions ISBN 978-1-62950-003-4 (PDF)
ISBN 978-1-62950-048-5 (EPUB)
ISBN 978-1-62950-049-2 (Mobi)

World Book, Inc.
180 North LaSalle Street
Suite 900
Chicago, Illinois 60601
U.S.A.

For information about other World Book publications, visit our website at
www.worldbook.com or call **1-800-967-5325**.

Printed in the United States of America by Mercury Print Productions, Rochester, New York

Contents

Foreword

Dr. Debbie Silver

Audiences who have had the privilege of watching veteran middle grades educator Jack Berckemeyer present have dubbed him "the funniest person in education." I think they are absolutely correct. With his hilarious characterizations of both students and the adults who teach them, Jack can bring me to tears of laughter with his spot-on observations. Thankfully, he is able to bring his wit and incredible insight to a larger stage through his book, *Taming of the Team*. With his irreverent asides and delightful anecdotes, he is able to infuse his humor into the important topic of teaming.

Jack's background as a teacher and consultant, along with his experience as the past Assistant Executive Director of the National Middle School Association, now Association for Middle Level Education (AMLE), give him a unique appreciation for the importance of teaming. This book outlines many configurations of what teams can look like and discusses variations on how teams can function in a school setting.

Jack offers administrators the support and tools they need in order to promote the idea of teaming, to make initial selections for the team configurations, to foster ongoing team development, to provide flexible scheduling for teams, and to make needed changes to dysfunctional teams. His belief is that without strong leadership, teams cannot function effectively and student needs cannot be met.

Other topics addressed include timely subjects such as how to use teams to address the Common Core State Standards, how to set up Google Docs™ for capturing group information, and how to use the 3-5-3 plan for dealing with student discipline issues. Jack emphasizes the importance of team agendas, team communication, and team unity. And he provides helpful pointers on how to achieve maximum benefit from all three.

Included with the book are several timesaving "print ready" questionnaires and forms for teams to use immediately, as well as an extensive survey to assess team effectiveness at the end of the year. A thorough Discussion Guide is provided at the end of the book to facilitate important conversations teammates need to have with each other.

You will also find uproarious "scientific surveys" and "meeting tips," as Jack adds the important aspect of funniness to the sometimes-difficult task of getting adults to work together. His satirical insights are tempered with a tolerance for human frailties, and his self-deprecating humor helps us put aside our pettiness and celebrate our humanity.

(Note Jack's asides that appear in this type throughout the book.)

Taming of the Team is packed with suggestions on how to select, build, and maintain effective teams that focus on kids, curriculum, and professional development. Jack's willingness to discuss his own journey, both the successes and not-so-successful team experiences he encountered, adds to our sense of "being there" as he outlines the essentials of creating a positive team environment. As a quintessential advocate for middle level learners, he never lets us forget the reason for having teams—to provide unwavering support for student welfare.

Jack Berckemeyer's book is a gift we teachers should give ourselves. With your team, read it, have fun with it, discuss it, refer to it, study it, set your goals using it, assess yourselves from it, and at the end of the year read it again and remember why you became a team in the first place.

Introduction

I remember going to the circus as a child. All the sights and sounds—the towering tent, a crowd of clowns cavorting, and the taste of the cotton candy as I licked my sticky fingers—are real in my memory. I can still feel the excitement centered in the three rings. Performers and animals moved at a dizzying pace. Acrobats tumbled and danced from ring to ring, animals pranced and plodded with precision, and strange machines that could shoot a human across the tent were assembled and dismantled before my very eyes. What a spectacle!

In many ways the circus of my childhood is very much like a school. Maybe at times the school doesn't run with the precision of a circus, but there is always some organization to the movement, noise, and commotion. And the performers—well, you might consider school teachers, students, and administrators performers on parade.

Watch as the aerialists take their positions above the center ring. The circus crew raises a net below them in case they fall as they fly from one trapeze to another. Could it be a team of teachers providing a safety net as students try out their wings? See the crowd of clowns stumbling out of the tiny car and filling the ring with joyous energy. Could it be a class of young adolescents exploding out of the classroom at the sound of the bell?

And then there are the lions and their tamer. I remember the anticipation I felt as a boy when the lions entered the ring. They were a sight to see—wild, majestic, powerful, and even scary. Yet, at times they seemed gentle and graceful.

Some days when I walk into a team meeting, I picture myself walking into the circus ring with the lions. On my team there are powerful individuals—some snarling at each other, some silently slinking by—and yet, the group must perform together for an anxious audience. Will the performance be well organized—graceful in its efficiency—or will it be wild and out of control?

Taming of the Team

Are you with me in this metaphor? You see, working with my team of teachers is like being in the center ring with a bunch of lions. Remember the lion that spends most of the time growling loudly, interrupting the act with the disturbance? That lion is the teacher with the biggest problem of the day. Imagine that teacher's complaints as angry growls. Watch the teacher strut around for a few minutes to mark his territory.

At the opposite end of the "cage" is a pair of docile lions. They are just going through the motions hoping for everything to end quickly so they can go back to their personal lives. We have all witnessed these team members. They have no desire to make waves. They just sit back waiting for someone else to step up or make a mistake during the meeting. They don't cause any problems, but they attend the gathering to see what is happening.

Look around your "lion's cage." Is there one lion that enters reluctantly or comes in late as the lion tamer cracks the whip? Do you see the lion that spends most of the time looking around and is continually off task? This lion seems confused—not sure of the routines and acting a little lost. This lion will probably ask a question that has already been asked or seem curious about everything. It is difficult to convince lions like this one to move. And when you *do* get them to move, they often head in the wrong direction.

Oh, and don't miss the "lions" that like to perform for the crowd. They do everything right. They are on cue and never miss a beat. They enjoy the praise and the applause. You'll find them in the center of the cage.

Sharing the center spotlight is the leader (or lion tamer) cracking a whip to keep the show moving along and everyone on task. Without this leader, the performance might become something of a feeding frenzy.

Look—it's time for the most amazing feat! The lion tamer lays the whip aside, stares into the eyes of the largest lion, cautiously opens its mouth, and places her head inside.

The head-in-the-lion's-mouth trick is a symbol of ultimate risk taking. Team leaders take big risks, too. True, they may never experience lion saliva firsthand, but they *are* asked to make tough decisions, take risks, crack the whip, and entertain crowds on a daily basis.

The Art of Taming Something

We can't watch a lion-taming act without being awed by the precision and timing. We instinctively know that the taming and teamwork in the center ring has taken hours of work and practice. Yet, in many cases, educators never consider taking time to tame a team. Instructional teams in our schools are expected to perform flawlessly without training. Teams and leaders need ongoing support, and every team needs long-term professional development.

Ten years ago, many schools spent time on team training, only to let their professional development model whither away. It is unusual to see schools go back to the basics and retrain new teachers and staff on the importance of teaming. Why? The answer is simple—new initiatives, new mandates, and new district expectations. Imagine what would happen if the lion tamer introduced several new lions to the act, but didn't bother to train them. It's common sense that the result would be less than satisfactory—possibly even chaos! Teachers know that to implement successful teaming, there must be a long-term focus on teaming that provides quality resources and training—not just a once-every-five-year training that is soon forgotten.

Creating change and reform in middle level education starts with the teams. They are the backbone of the middle school. Middle school teachers are the fearless lions that might roar, wander, or even strut their stuff; but in the end they are responsible for the best part of the show.

Use this book as a resource to reinvent or establish your school teams. *Taming of the Team* will focus on how to make sure that your teams spend their time on kids, curriculum, and professional development. I will provide real examples to help move teams forward, to fortify the foundations of teaming, and offer new insights for encouraging effective teams. I might even throw in some funny references and stories to help make the text come alive because—let's admit it—sometimes people in schools can take themselves a little too seriously.

Taming a team is hard work. It takes dedication, strong leadership with a commitment to the foundation provided by the teaming concept, and teachers who believe in teaming and want to work together.

Take a risk. Put your head into the mouth of the lion. Just remember, middle school is like the Big Top Circus—full of fun and surprises.

Defining Teaming

A critical element to successful middle schools is to create small, personalized learning communities by implementing interdisciplinary teaming. Teaming creates a context that enables students and teachers to better know one another, and allows teachers to better understand and support the learning of students. Teams generally focus on creating coordinated lesson plans; discussing student progress, problems, and issues; and integrating curricula and instruction. The growing body of evidence supporting the positive impact of interdisciplinary teaming on middle grades schools and students is difficult to refute. Students and teachers in schools that have implemented teaming and its associated practices with some degree of integrity consistently report more positive and productive learning environments. In addition, more large-scale and comprehensive studies have been conducted that successfully demonstrate the positive effects of teaming on student [achievement] outcomes.

Steven B. Mertens & Nancy Flowers

Bringing a common group of students and teachers together helps foster communication and allows teachers to really get to know their students. This common group shares common experiences and helps tackle the daily tasks of school work. The group also shares a common vision and makes sure all decisions are in the best interests of their students. These groups are consistent in their policies and procedures and have a common mission statement that allows for student input and growth. This group is a team.

For many teams the mantra is simple—same teachers, same kids, one common goal.

• Teams Help Students and Teachers See Connections

Teams are designed to bring subjects together, so teachers can work with others outside of their subject areas. This allows teachers and students to see connections in curriculum and provides flexibility to connect content where appropriate. The goals of every true team should be about kids, curriculum, and professional development. If teams focus their energy on these elements, no one will ever question the legitimacy of teaming within the middle school.

• Teams Make a Large School Feel Small

Teaming helps make schools feel smaller. There are many large schools across the world, most of them in the United States. Some have more than 2,500 students. There are even grade-level buildings with more than 2,000 students. Without question, some of these schools are too large.

In many cases, schools that large could launch themselves into outer space with the energy and hormones that are produced within their walls.

Many experts say that the best size for a middle school is around 700–1,100 students. A school that size can have full electives and full class offerings with little or no sharing of teachers. However, very seldom do districts make decisions on what is developmentally appropriate. They tend to make decisions on what is economically feasible. As schools unfortunately become larger, we need ways to make them feel smaller, and teams do that every day.

These big schools beg for teaming. Because the teachers and the kids in a team are working toward the same purpose, they are building a community, and parents see that a group of teachers really understands and cares about their children.

• Great Teams Increase Student Advocacy and Focus on Achievement

If teams spend time talking about all of the students on their teams, student achievement will rise. There are several ways to make sure teams are focused on students. Think of the results that can happen when a whole group of adults focuses on the same group of kids! They can really get to know the students—who they are and what they need as individuals and as a group. Everybody will be working together to provide what's best for this lucky selection of students. Together, they see that no student is left on the edges.

Second, the team can make sure each student has not only a team surrounding them and providing support, but also one special adult advocate who has a particular focus on him or her. This advocate checks in regularly with that student and helps to ensure success—making sure the student completes work, gets questions answered, finishes homework, completes all assignments, and feels noticed.

> Right! How can a team make sure they are talking about every single student? On page 138 I've outlined a way to do this. The idea isn't original to me. I was lucky to see my good friend Kathy Hunt Ullock work with various teams across the world. One of the best strategies she used was an activity called "Thumbs Up, Thumbs Down." This activity ensures that team members think about each student during the team meeting.

• Teaming Is Not Just for Middle Schools

Teaming and professional learning communities (PLCs) are blossoming all over the world. In East Chicago, Indiana, schools are teaming in grades 7–12. In Sandusky, Ohio, Perkins Local and Sandusky schools are teaming in grades 9 and 10. They focus on kids, curriculum, and professional development. They do their own discipline plans and meet with students on a regular basis. They are discussing their curriculum. Teams in all grade levels are spending time doing academic and behavioral plans for individualized students, and they are working on teacher consistency issues.

Elementary schools are also working in professional learning communities. They are meeting to discuss student data, work on educational plans, plan curriculum, and meet with parents as a team. Great schools know the value of teaming. They just struggle with how to make sure teams use the time effectively.

Teaming is not just a middle school concept. It is a smart idea for teachers and administrators of all levels, for parents, and for students. The goal for all schools should be to figure out how to make sure teachers have the time to meet and work together. With limited school budgets and more accountability, teachers need this team time more than ever.

The Truth About Teaming

Over the years, educators have referred to teaming as *professional study groups, professional learning communities, data teams,* and *learning teams*. There are vertical teams, horizontal teams, elective teams, exploratory teams, academic teams, and leadership teams. Yet, no matter what you call teaming, it is really just about a group of people coming together. It is not about the name, it is about the purpose of coming together. That purpose is to improve all facets of the school experience, including academic performance, for all students.

Teaming Takes Training and Caring

By all accounts, one of the most important aspects of the middle level concept is teaming, and one fact remains the same: Quality training for teams is essential but often gets left in the dust when a new fad or phrase comes along.

- Hundreds of articles have been written about teaming's foundations and the research that supports teaming. (See the Research Points in the Resources, page 139, for more information.)
- A massive amount of time has been spent teaching middle level educators to work together. Current research supports the need for teams and the importance of effective use of team time.

Many of the schools I work with did a great job of training teachers on teaming in the late 1980's or 1990's, but they failed to revisit this training as new teachers joined existing teams. They also assumed these new teachers and teachers who taught other grade levels understood and embraced teaming.

Teams can do great things. Take a look at the types of teams that have won the Teams That Make A Difference Awards, sponsored by Pearson and the Association for Middle Level Education (AMLE), formerly National Middle School Association. Or read *Teamwork* by Monique Wild, Amanda Mayeaux, and Kathryn Edmonds. This book highlights the successful journey of a team—a team so successful that they won the Disney American Teacher Award. There are hundreds of examples of how great teams daily are doing amazing things in their schools.

Teaming Takes Sharp Leadership

Without great teams, schools would flounder and never succeed. It takes a lot of time and energy to get teams to be successful. Most importantly, it takes a great school leader who will commit to the teaming process and stay the course with long-term professional development. It is not an easy task to stay focused on teams when there are so many changes and mandates that occur so fast. About the time you get everyone on the same page, someone has written a new chapter, and you are expected to move on. A great team leader supplies the team with the tools necessary to grow and evolve. Great leaders seek out new curriculum and interesting ways to involve teams in professional development within the school.

Not only will effective school leaders look for outstanding teaming curriculum, but they will also shake up teams when necessary and encourage existing teams that they are moving in the right direction. Without this leadership and strong internal support, outsiders question why teams are important to successful schools.

For some superintendents, school board members, and other teachers in the district, there is a perception that the cost of teaming in a school is not necessary. This is not a new argument. For years, educators have heard the same old cry from school leaders who do not understand the power of real teaming.

- "It's just another prep time for teachers."
- "I wish I had more time to do nothing."
- "Half of those teachers don't even like each other!"
- "What are teachers really doing in those teams?"
- "Why are teams spending 95% of their time on the same 5% of their students?"
- "Does teaming really affect academic achievement?"

In some cases where a team is not using its time effectively, these questions and comments are valid. And in some instances schools need to make the necessary changes within teams.

Yet for every documented horror story about teaming, there are millions of success stories. Yes, sometimes teams struggle, argue, waste valuable time, or fail to meet. But that is not the case if the school leader is a true advocate for teaming.

Teaming Takes Focus on the Big Three

With today's emphasis on high-stakes testing, accountability, and decreasing school budgets, schools and teams are being held to a higher standard—a standard that mandates teams to focus on kids, curriculum, and professional development. If teams take the time to use these three focal points as their guideposts, teaming will find its true purpose in today's schools.

Teaming really comes down to what each of the team members brings to the table. Great teams have people who want to contribute, want to make a difference in student achievement, and want to improve the school community. Teaming is about creating an environment that makes the students comfortable with a small group of teachers, yet be able to grow out of the elementary self-contained classroom.

Todd Fielding
Subject Area Lead Teacher for Social Studies
8th-grade Civics Teacher
Eagle Ridge Middle School
Ashburn, VA

*A Special Chapter for Administrators with
Tips and Strategies for Creating Teams*

Creating Teams

*Great teams start with a combination of the right teachers
and the right students.*

Judith Baenen

One of the hardest tasks an administrator will do in his or her educational career is to create teams. In many cases this can be a lose-lose situation. It can be frustrating and even result in a few gray hairs over the long ordeal. However, with some time and energy, great administrators can work out all the pieces and create a fantastic plan that brings teachers together in amazing teams.

Don't take the task of creating teams for granted. It takes time, research, planning, and a ton of risk. There are so many factors that must be explored and discussed. Many of the factors relate to the highly qualified teacher provisions of the *No Child Left Behind* law. There are issues of federal and state mandates, certification, standards, curriculum configurations—all of which can be mind-boggling for the administrator, teachers, and district personnel. If you are assigned the task of creating teams, open the lion's mouth and insert your head!

Part of being a leader is to make the tough decisions and work with your staff to help implement those decisions. Yes, leadership is about risks, but when those risks are good for kids and teams they are the right risks to take!

*Paul Destino
Principal
Mayfield Middle School, Mayfield Heights, Ohio*

There are several ways to create a team. In many cases, the more input you elicit and the more people you involve in the process, the better.

Here are some strategies to help create a team:

- Survey the staff about whom they would like to work with for the next several years. Make sure they justify their answers. Just as when middle school kids are placed in group learning situations, it is not about "being with a friend."

- Chart teacher strengths and select teams based on these strengths.

- Create a committee to help formalize teams. This allows for teacher buy-in and support in the teaming process.

- Take time to ask teachers why they would not work with a certain faculty member. Reasons need to be based on philosophical issues. Because a teacher once ate another teacher's yogurt is not a philosophical issue.

- Map out teachers' certification areas and grade level certifications, then start putting the pieces together.

- Look for personality strengths and areas of weakness.

- Check astronomy charts to see if teachers are aligned. You may need a little something strange to help put the pieces together.

- Try to create smaller teams for younger grade levels. This helps with transition issues.

- Decide how to involve the elective teachers (or as I call them, essentials teachers) as part of a team. Some middle schools choose to create an essentials team. However, this can create a scheduling issue. If creating an essentials team is difficult due to traveling teacher issues or part-time teachers, at least consider what to do with the essentials teachers who are there all day. You can even create smaller essentials teams based on the schedule and classes. There could be a technology team and an arts team. The essentials teams could be grouped into humanities, fine arts, and applied arts teams. (There's more on this issue in Chapter 8.)

Changing Existing Teams

For those administrators who are thinking about moving teams just to change things up, consider these questions:

1. Are the teams in the building working effectively?

2. Have the teams taken on a negative personality?

3. Is the reason for changing the teams to hide a poor or inadequate teacher?

4. Is there an unhealthy team?

5. What outcomes do I expect when I change the teams?

6. Do I really want to do this?

7. Will the teams help increase student achievement and parent involvement?

8. Will the new teams improve student relationships?

Evaluate the answers to these questions before you take the giant leap into the wild world of changing up teams. This leap can truly make or break a school environment. And it can make or break a principal.

If you decide to make team changes, spend time preparing the staff for the change. Ask team members for input and spend time explaining the final process. Change can be very hard for the teachers, and many may remain bitter for years unless they are part of the process and are informed during the decision-making process.

Sometimes Teams Require Changes

> *There are some teams that have become institutionalized in our schools and become very competitive. For example, one 8th grade team might have a unit on zoology, while another team might say, "We are going to the zoo!" Another team might say, "Well, we are bringing in Jack Hanna." And the last team would simply say, "We are going to Africa!"*
>
> *Kathy Hunt Ullock*
> *Middle Level Consultant*

When teams are not working together and become divisive, school leaders will need to break up and reconfigure the groups.

The rule of thumb is that teams need at least three to five years to really come together and make progress. It is not until year seven that teams start to take on the biggest personality. In some cases, that big personality may not be positive and then suddenly the whole team becomes negative. When that happens, teams need to be separated for the benefit of the kids and for the adults on the team.

Before you rearrange teams, consider these rules:

1. Have a plan
2. Consult staff
3. Review certifications of teachers
4. Solicit retirements (Just kidding!)
5. Consider all the options in creating a team
6. Have teams evaluate their past performances

Always know that making team changes can be full of mistakes and challenges and can have a negative impact on the school; but it can also be the breath of fresh air that is needed for the students and teachers.

Creating teams is like putting on a show. It can be frustrating, but when the last piece fits you are overjoyed and there is a big sigh of relief. Just like the three-ring circus: When it all comes together, it can be an amazing sight to see!

In the end, when the teams are announced and put into place, it's funny how teachers can act like middle level students who are not happy with a decision or policy. Remember the Big Top Circus analogy, "The show must go on!"

Becoming a Team

God didn't create self-contained classrooms, 50-minute periods, and subjects taught in isolation. We did—because sometimes we find working alone safer and easier than working together.

Roland Barth

Few educators publicly assert that working in isolation is the best strategy for improving schools. Instead, they give reasons why it is impossible for them to work together. "We just can't find the time." "Not everyone on the staff has endorsed the idea." "We need more training in collaboration." But the number of schools that have created truly collaborative cultures proves that such barriers are not insurmountable.

Rick DuFour

Just as trapeze artists must trust the workers who man the equipment and set up the nets, so must team members learn to trust each other. One of the main issues and concerns for teams is how to remain consistent and create unity among the teachers and students. Teaming is all about the importance of a group of people coming together for a common mission or cause. It is about developing the ability to trust one another and work together toward a common purpose.

For those of us in middle school, a common goal is to not let students carry out a hostile takeover! Let's be honest here; at any given time we are just 40 seconds away from having our class turn into a scene from Lord of the Flies!

Teams Need Time to Get to Know Each Other

Once a team is created, they need time together. Great teams will meet in the summer prior to school. They might meet at a team member's house or a local establishment. The purpose is simple: to get to know each other.

It is critical to make sure you find time to talk about issues not related to school. Later, there will be plenty of opportunities to worry about progress reports, team celebrations, and who needs to bring doughnuts to the next team meeting.

Here are some ideas on what to do for the first meeting:

- Spend time talking about your teaching background.

- Talk about some of your teaching strategies.

- Share your pet peeves.

- Talk about family and why you became a teacher.

- List things you expect from your teammates. Share a great past team experience.

- Create a list of nonnegotiables for you and for your team.

- Conduct a fun survey that is not too serious. Magazines usually have light-hearted surveys, although you might not want to know if your team member is a good kisser.

- Keep the first meeting lighthearted and have plenty of food.
  Remember my motto—Eating makes a meeting!

- Bring in a copy of your photo when you were in middle school. Share a photo of yourself as a middle school student.
  Now let's see, where did I put those black and white photos?

Jack Berckemeyer, Grade 8

In his book, *The Personal Trainer for Academic Teams*, Randy Thompson emphasizes how critical it is for a team to work toward building an identity. This identity relates not only to students, but also to teachers. Randy suggests creating team banners, team resumes, and a team wall with information about the students *and* teachers.

Some teams list their degrees and accomplishments in their team area of the building. We should be proud of the hard work we have done and proud of the many hours we spend outside of the classroom increasing our knowledge.

Taking and Sharing Get-Acquainted Questionnaires

Doing some fun things to get acquainted is a great way to start the process of team bonding. One great way to start is to have all team members complete a slightly wacky questionnaire. Here are two examples, but you will certainly have fun designing your own.

Here's how you can use Questionnaire 1.

Give each team member a copy. After questionnaires are completed, shuffle the pages and redistribute them so that no one has his or her own paper.

Each team member reads a questionnaire and guesses whose answers these are. A teacher writes his or her guess on the page and passes it on. When the guessing spots are filled, keep passing papers until each one comes back around to the original writer.

Full-page version on page 140

Taming of the Team

Each member can share responses to his or her questionnaire. Or the team leader can read a completed paper and everyone can guess. Or team members can comment on one or two of their answers.

Here's how you can use Questionnaire 2.

Give each team member a copy. Each member completes one, writing ideas about which other member might fit each item.

As a group, members can share their ideas or responses to each item. It will be fun to hear reasoning behind their choices. Then individuals can talk about why others were right in guesses about them, or why they were not.

Full-page version on page 141

To wrap up, have each team member state one thing learned about every other team member.

Building Some Baseline Information

In addition to having some fun and getting to know one another, it is critical that teams take some time to build baseline data about their team's structure and their effective use of time.

During the fist few weeks of school, the team should work together to complete the two-page survey, "Where Are We?"

This allows the team to gather information about the current state of various policies and practices of the team.

The responses will indicate areas for team discussion. (Please note, you may not feel you need some of these strategies. Just make sure you discuss them as a team.)

If as a team you discover areas of weakness or identify missing strategies, create some goals. Feel free to add questions that relate specifically to your school or your team.

Full-page version on page 142

I encourage teams to take this informal survey at least four times a year. It will be interesting for team members to see how well the team is functioning at the beginning of the year versus the end of the year. Keep track of the data.

Administrators can also use this to keep track of the practices teams are implementing. This is not a checklist of things that every team must do. Present this to teams as a list of ideas that many great teams are implementing across the country.

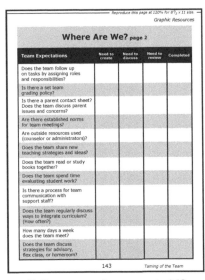

Full-page version on page 143

Nurturing Team Unity

Teamwork is the ability to work together toward a common vision—the ability to direct individual accomplishment toward organizational objectives. It is the fuel that allows common people to attain uncommon results.

Andrew Carnegie

Creating a Team Name

To encourage team unity, many teams and schools come up with team names. It is always interesting to ask teachers why they have team names. Many teachers just say it is something the school has been doing for years. Some are not sure why it happens. Some teams become so excited about their team name, they act like it is the name of their firstborn child.

Unfortunately, it seems that many middle level teachers have more of an ownership of their team's name than the students do. I once asked a teacher why her team was called the Jaguars, and she simply stated it was because she had a bunch of laminated posters featuring jaguars.

> We know how much teachers love to laminate things in the classroom. I think some teachers would laminate the classroom gerbil, if they could. But a laminated set of posters alone is not a good reason for naming a team.

Teams spend very little time asking students for their input. Yes, it takes time and energy to ask students about a team name, but student ownership comes with student input.

Here are some simple ways to get input and involve students in the process.

- Ask students for ideas during advisory or home base. Recognize the class with the greatest number of ideas and the class with the best ideas.

- Create a contest at the beginning of the year and offer a reward.

- Have kids create a team logo or shirt that can be used for the year.

- Some schools even retire old team names and place them on a banner in the school gym. This process is similar to a winning sports team or a record holder. Once the team name is displayed on the banner, another team can never use it.

- Have the students create a task force. That group can generate ideas and give a presentation to the entire team.

- Ask the staff to come up with a theme, then ask teams to create ideas from the common theme.

There is nothing wrong with being creative; just seek student input. You might be surprised what students can come up with when given a chance.

A team often creates an acronym for itself, like the S.T.A.R.S team or the C.R.A.P team, which stands for Caring, Responsible and Prepared (a fake name, but it sounds funny and makes me laugh).

Creating a Team Vision

At the beginning of the year take a few minutes to develop a team vision or mission that reflects your team characteristics and expectations. Don't forget to make sure that the mission is grade-level appropriate.

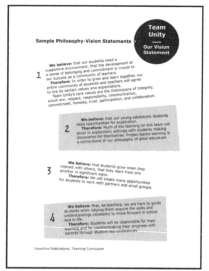

Full-page version on page 144

Make sure that your vision focuses on what will happen for the students. You can use the schoolwide mission statement as a starting point.

Great schools use the team mission or vision statements to help create a unified vision for the school. This is why it is imperative for teams to focus on quality statements. Remember to keep the statements simple.

Full-page version on page 145

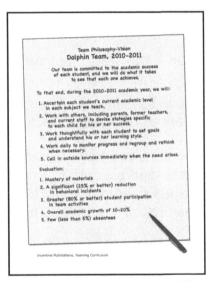

Full-page version on page 146

As a team, having a common vision and set of objectives for you and your students can help increase student achievement.

Becky Ruchti
Teacher
East Chicago City School, East Chicago, Indiana

Taming of the Team

Sharing Your Team Mission

Once the team has created a mission or vision statement, share it.

- Create a three-fold brochure for open house and share it with the parents on your team.

- Post the statement on the team website.

- Record your statement at the end of your voice mail.

- Post the statement in every classroom.

- Wait, make a T-shirt with the mission statement on it. Teachers adore the matching T-shirts.

- Make sure the statement is posted on the bulletin boards in your hallway.

- See if the statement can be printed on the grade sheets or progress reports.

- Have students put the team's mission in their student planner or agenda books.

Making sure you have a common vision allows the teachers, students, and parents to know that this team has a goal in mind. It reminds everyone that there is purpose to this team and that the team is trying to accomplish great things.

Agreeing on Norms for Team Meetings

In order to keep a team on task and focused, you will need to establish some team expectations and norms for team members to follow at team meetings. Be realistic and honest about issues that may arise. It is truly okay to say that at no time during the team meeting is it acceptable to work on your tax return!

You can negotiate these norms without hurting team members' feelings. Stick to the topics and stay on point. Work together to answer the question, "What are the acceptable actions during a team meeting?"

Great teams review their team norms quarterly. This reminds everyone of the expectations and enables teams to make reasoned adjustments. Teams also make sure the lists of norms are posted in the team room, team notebook, or conference area.

Examples of Team Norms

- Be on time for the meeting.

- Never grade papers during a team meeting.

- Let the person talking finish his or her statement or thought.

- Bring any materials that you will need. Yes, that includes a pen and paper. Don't be an unprepared student!

- When the meeting is over it is over, don't talk about it with others. Teaming is like Las Vegas—what happens in team meetings stays in team meetings.

- Maintain all student communication logs and parent contacts.

- Respond to team and parent e-mails within 24 hours.

- Share teaching ideas and student data with others.

- Bring your homework dates and lesson plans.

- Set team time and locations.

Believe it or not, having a set place to meet makes a huge difference. Try to find a neutral location if possible. Teacher classrooms are oozing with distractions for teachers. You can always find a project to do in your own room, which distracts others and the team meeting.

Seek a place that is private and has access to a computer, phone, and copy machine if possible. I truly understand that in many of our schools space is limited, and we are just grateful to have a classroom. A team meeting room in some cases is a luxury!

Keeping Up with Everyday Teamwork

Individual commitment to a group effort—that is what makes a team work, a company work, a society work, a civilization work.

Vince Lombardi

Coming together is a beginning. Keeping together is progress. Working together is success.

Henry Ford

Team Members' Roles and Responsibilities

Once a team has begun to function as a unified group, it must not neglect dividing the roles and responsibilities necessary to keep it functioning. Think about your teammates' personal characteristics as roles within the team are assigned. Make sure the assignment is suited to a member's strengths. Feel free to rotate many of the roles and responsibilities. Teachers do get bored with the same old dull routines. Take a look at a list of roles that need to be filled on a team:

- Team leader
- Recorder
- Parent contact
- Advisory liaison
- Newsletter editor
- Webmaster
- Homework hotline or e-mail blitz guru
- Communicator with the elective and exploratory teachers
- Contact for the school guidance office
- Someone who brings treats and snacks (Remember eating makes a meeting!)
- Planner for events, birthdays, and celebrations

Team roles and responsibilities really do help a team grow and function. They allow teachers to complete tasks and remain focused on kids, curriculum, and professional development.

Team Calendar

Create a team calendar that highlights all major projects, due dates, end-of-year reports, progress-report due dates, and any other team-related important dates. Keep this in the team meeting area. Make the calendar large enough for everyone to see. Maintain or update it on a weekly basis.

A great team also posts its team calendar on the team website, in the team notebook, and in the team meeting room. The team sends a monthly calendar home to parents about the upcoming events and projects. This helps communicate homework assignments, field trips, and project due dates.

Keep it simple and informative. Team calendars help students, parents, and even the most absent-minded teacher.

Monday	Tuesday	Wednesday	Thursday	Friday
LANGUAGE ARTS PROJECT DUE	AFTERSCHOOL MAKE-UP WORK DAY	BRING YOUR KID TO WORK DAY	SCIENCE QUIZ	MATH ASSESSMENT
ASSEMBLY ON ASTHMA	SOCIAL STUDIES POSTER DUE	MATH FRACTION TEST	READING ASSESSMENT	INTERVENTION AND ENHANCEMENT DAY
ANTI-BULLYING PROJECT DUE	ADVISORY TEAMS VISITING LOCAL ELEMENTARY SCHOOL	AFTERSCHOOL MAKE-UP DAY		TEAM AWARDS CELEBRATION
	LANGUAGE ARTS VOCABULARY TEST	TEAM SKATE NIGHT		

Team Rewards

Teams are constantly looking for ways to motivate students. There is an interesting debate about how often and how much we should reward students. In her book, *Fall Down 7 Times, Get Up 8*, Dr. Debbie Silver observes, "There is no single right answer when dealing with rewards. Sometimes less is more." I think Debbie is correct: It is not about the quantity, it is about the quality of the team rewards.

We know that young adolescents crave adult interactions. Maybe team lunches with the teachers and one-on-one time with a teacher are enough for a student reward. In many cases, young adolescents are seeking someone just to listen to them. It is not about candy and extra bonus points.

> Let's be honest, if a student likes you and likes the class, she or he will work for dirt in a cup.

I encourage teams to look closely at how rewards such as stars, stickers, and bonus points impact a student's work ethic. I do believe in praise for students. I believe simple things like a warm smile and a slight "thumbs up" do help, but do rewards increase achievement and comprehension? True comprehension and academic success come from hard work, dedication, and time.

> Maybe a team could look for ways to honor those characteristics, instead of trying to figure out how we can give Emily a certificate for being the best glue eater in the class.

Team Celebrations

Great teams look for unique ways to celebrate the students on the team. There are teams that will do monthly celebrations with the entire team. Find an open area in your school and make that your team celebration area. Use a bulletin board to post snapshots, sample student writing, or artwork.

Here is a great list of other team celebrations:

- Birthdays

- Project celebrations for outstanding work on a class project

- Good citizenship awards

- Helping those who help others award

- Outside-of-school accomplishments such as 4H, sports teams, or dance presentations

- Participation in sports—hold a tailgate party for your students before a home basketball game or football game

- Grade-changing award—honor students who have increased their grades for the quarter

- Student who has the best smelling deodorant—I am checking to see if you are paying attention.

- On time and ready award—for students who come prepared for class

- "Hey that was nice," award—given when students do nice things for each other

- Thought-provoking award—given when a student says something that is profound and interesting

- Stumped-the-teacher award—given when a student comes up with an answer that even the teacher did not predict

- Best artist or cartoonist award

- Technology support award—given for students who help other kids with computer issues or technology issues

- Top of the line award—for students who are always polite and kind

- Celebration for all homework completed by the class

- Everyone passed an objective celebration

- End of testing celebration

- Giving celebration—if a student gives to someone else, they can attend a party or celebration

- Celebration for a month of no tardies

Adult Celebrations

There are so many great ways to help teams celebrate. Don't forget, it is important to take time to honor each other as adults. Make sure that as adults, you celebrate birthdays and life-changing events. Yes, everyone on the team may not love the fun, but it does build unity and morale.

Teams can honor teachers on the team by celebrating:

- Teacher becoming Nationally Board Certified

- Team member getting married or divorced (if it is a joyous occasion)

- Team member birthday

- Team member being honored as an outstanding teacher by their local newspaper or TV station

- Teacher who is chosen teacher of the month or year in the school, district, state, or nation

- Teacher who is going to a sporting state tournament as a coach or official

- Births of children, grandchildren, or great grandchildren (maybe even great, great, great grandchildren!)

Setting Consistent Expectations

*How many different procedures does a 12-year-old
have to deal with in a day?*

Jack Berckemeyer

I was never an advocate for a list of team expectations. The real
reason was simple. I had created *Mr. Berckemeyer's Alphabet
Book*. The book highlighted my list of five classroom examples
per letter of the alphabet. For example,

> *A* means always be on time.
> *B* means be polite.

The list was never ending. I am sure the alphabet book was
the sole reason students came to sixth grade. I know they
went home at the end of the day and memorized all 5,000
expectations I had for each and every one of them. I used
this alphabet book for several years.

I will never forget when my teammates came to me one year
and said, "Jack, we need to be more consistent."

I answered, "Yes, you do." Another phrase I learned to regret.
I told them I had my list of expectations and felt that it worked
for me.

Well, not six days after the conversation with my teammates,
I began to notice a young man from my sixth grade class go
into the restroom and then walk out fairly quickly. I thought to
myself, "I know he is not flushing the toilet, and he is not
washing his hands." So being a good teacher, I told him that he
needed to flush the toilet and wash his hands when he used the
restroom. He replied that he didn't go to the bathroom to use

Taming of the Team

the restroom. He said, "In your alphabet book, you said we had to go to the bathroom before we came to your class." Once again, I was duped by a 10-year-old.

I started to realize that my list was for me—not for my team, and not for the benefit of my students. So I walked into my team meeting and informed my team that I was ready to create a list of team expectations for our students. The concern that I had was making sure that the list was no larger than five or six items. We are talking about young adolescents. My alphabet book had shown me that the list could be too long.

I just needed to make sure that the list contained my personal pet peeve. To some of you this pet peeve might seem trivial or even crazy, but to me it's a big deal. I am not a fan of kids sitting on the tops of their desks. It drives me crazy, and I think it rude. The hard part was trying to convince my teammates that this was a legitimate issue.

After exerting a vast amount of time and energy with me demonstrating real-life examples of the perils of sitting on top of a desk, my teammates agreed not to allow kids to sit on top of their desks. I know they thought I was a freak, but victory was mine!

We discovered some other common procedures, and consistency within our team was enhanced.

Creating a List of Expectations

Effective teams spend time creating consistency for their students by developing routines such as:

- How to enter the room
- What to do when class is over
- Handing in homework
- Late work

- Earning bonus points
- Writing a heading on papers
- Using hall passes
- Many of the other issues that help with organization

Have you ever taken time as a team and written down all the classroom expectations for all the different teachers that a middle school student on your team faces during the day?

The list can be endless. So as you develop a consistent policy with your team and introduce the list to your students, focus on three to five expectations at a time. In this case, it is about quality, not about quantity.

> *When teams have consistency, students will live up to the expectations. However, if adults cannot even coordinate simple tasks like what the heading on the paper should include, then how do we expect our students to really be ready to learn?*
>
> *Bonnie Wicker*
> *8th Grade Teacher*
> *Lima West, Lima, Ohio*

As you create your list, please note there are some expectations that should *not* be on the list. Take a look at a few examples.

1. Raise your hand
2. Don't talk when others are talking
3. Be respectful
4. Be kind
5. Help others

These are examples of life expectations that are enforced throughout the year. These are skills required to be a good human being. They are character education components. Your list of expectations should be about items that are expected by teachers to help maintain the organization of the classroom.

Also, start with easy ones like putting the heading on a paper. You want to experience success. Take your time and work through the expectations and the consequences for the students. Work toward the more difficult items such as grading policies and late work.

One way to point out the existing inconsistencies is to do a simple exercise where each team member explains his or her personal expectations on a given topic.

Here are two examples.

TEACHER	CLASS	LIST OF EXPECTATIONS
Heading on a Paper		
MS. TRUMBO	SPECIAL EDUCATION	FIRST NAME ONLY
MR. BERCKEMEYER	LANGUAGE ARTS	NAME, DATE, AND PERIOD RIGHT-HAND CORNER
MR. GASSMAN	SCIENCE	FIRST NAME
MS. TOSSAVA	SOCIAL STUDIES	FIRST AND LAST NAME RIGHT-HAND CORNER OF THE PAPER
Late Work		
MS. TRUMBO	SPECIAL EDUCATION	ACCEPTS ALL WORK UNTIL TWO DAYS BEFORE THE END OF THE QUARTER
MR. BERCKEMEYER	LANGUAGE ARTS	TAKE ALL WORK UNTIL TWO DAYS BEFORE THE END OF THE QUARTER, TAKES 10% OFF FOR BEING LATE
MR. GASSMAN	SCIENCE	10% OFF FOR EVERY DAY IT IS LATE
MS. TOSSAVA	SOCIAL STUDIES	TAKE ALL WORK UNTIL TWO DAYS BEFORE THE END OF THE QUARTER— 10% OFF FOR BEING LATE

Create a complete chart of expectations, analyze the chart, and then find commonalities. See if there are areas where the team is already consistent. Then look for ways to compromise and become more consistent for the benefit of the students.

The reality is that everyone on the team might have different expectations for late work. You could have one person that believes it is late right after it is collected and another person on your team that might say, "As long as it is handed in by the end of the universe, I will give them credit." Therefore, start simple and work towards the big stuff.

The hard part will be remaining consistent within the team. The students will live up to the expectations—the people that will not live up to the expectations will be you and your teammates. For example, you might have an expectation about not sitting on the top of desks, like I do. Everyone on your team might agree to that expectation. However, during passing period you might walk by a teammate's room and see a student sitting on the top of the desk. Observing this lack of respect for the expectation causes several emotions. First anger, then spite, and ultimately the desire for revenge. So you either badmouth Mr. Toombs behind his back or ignore him for a period of time.

What usually happens in this case is that students then come into your room and proceed to sit on the top of the desk.
You say, "Get off the desk!"

They say, "Mr. Toombs lets us!"

You say, "Do I look like Mr. Toombs? Am I wearing a hairpiece and an ugly beard?"

This is a case of educational sabotage (and not a good idea, of course). During team meeting time, members need to remind each other of the expectations and ask each other, "Why are we not supporting the list of expectations?"

Here is the deal: As teachers we confront parents, kids, or our administrators as long as two other people come with us! The hardest person to confront is a fellow teacher. In many cases, we just remain bitter and angry. I know teachers who have carried a grudge about another teacher for years. Let it go! There are so many people against us as educators. *Let's not turn on each other.*

We have to learn that good teaming involves some dialogue and some conflict. It takes work and good communication to remain consistent. It also takes effort and the ability to be honest with each other. If we remain consistent with each other, it will help us stay on the same page. We know that middle school students want some consistency in their turbulent lives. We can provide that by creating some basic policies and procedures. This might even help decrease classroom interruptions and the need to repeat everything over and over again.

> Remember—the most inconsistent person in the room is almost always the teacher!

Making Decisions Together

> *My team is made up of five individuals who are as different as people can be: the strong-silent type, the tension breaker, the hard baller, the nurturer, and the by-the-booker. Obviously, these variations cause their fair share of head butting and frustration. However, we're all professionals and we are all exceptional at what we do. The best thing about our dynamics is the fact that we all have our strengths and weaknesses. We're all going to have our bad days, but there is only a minuscule chance of anything slipping by all of us. Each one of us is a safety net for the other four. There is at least one of us with whom each student can identify, a task with which each of us deals well, and five different approaches for every challenge that we may face.*
>
> *Jason M. Williams*
> *Washington Middle School*
> *English Teacher - Team Inspiration*

It is funny how important it is for teachers, teams, parents, students, and administrators to come to consensus when dealing with an issue.

The fact is, I am not sure we will ever have complete consensus in education—at least not until I am Ruler of Education. Being Ruler of Education would allow me to make immediate changes that are based on what is right for students. I would establish a forum where we as educators were responsible for policing our own. Educators would not tolerate bad teaching. We would be allowed to vote our fellow teachers *off the island* if they were rude or disrespectful to kids, parents, or other teachers. I recently shared my desire to be Ruler of Education with friends and they said, "I would vote for you, Jack!" I quickly responded by saying, "If I am ruler, you don't vote!"

Consensus for a person like me is difficult. I see things the way I see them. I can be aggressive and assertive at times. I tend to not want to back off on my position, and I have been known to be a bully at times. I can even beat the dead horse until it is reincarnated! So for me, consensus is not an easy process, and for many educators, coming to consensus is a struggle. (Do you have some on your team?)

Researchers and educators have developed numerous great models for facilitating the consensus process. For individual teams, the first step is to make sure that at least you have a process.

I am a simple person. I tend to just appreciate when a teammate looks me in the eye and asks, "Well, what can you live with?" How many times in your career did you wish that someone would just ask you what you could live with? It is better than someone trying to verbally beat you down with more examples and the guilt trip about how you don't care about kids. Knowing what a person can live with allows you to come to a starting point.

Once you have a starting point you can move forward, or at least realize what will work and what needs more time. Every person is different in how they come to a conclusion or decision. Here are some typical personalities that teams need to consider as they choose their consensus model.

- **The Thinker**

  Thinkers tend to take a period of time to consider options and ramifications. They process all the information and try to come to a solid decision. This could take them anywhere from a day to 52 weeks.

- **The Quick-to-Judgment Person**

  These teachers have an answer right away. They have made up their mind until someone convinces them otherwise. They voice their thoughts immediately and can talk about an issue forever.

- **The Waffler**

  Wafflers see every side of the story and can never come up with one answer. They make statements like, "Well, if we do this . . . ."

- **The I-Don't-Commit Person**

  These people do not want their name next to anything. They don't like to take risks, and in many cases, did not even hear the question.

- **The Dazed-and-Confused Group**

  These dazed-and-confused individuals are in the media center waiting for the meeting that started 20 minutes ago in the science room, so they are no help in decision making.

It is hard to come to consensus when there are so many different personalities. Just getting everyone on the same page and focused is a challenge—that is why great teams have a plan and an established process for making decisions.

During a team meeting, spend a few minutes role-playing a "decision needed" scenario. Approach the scenario as if it were a decision that your team needed to make immediately. Discuss the scenario and come to a decision as to what your team would do. Then reflect on your team's decision-making process. Try to identify what happened. Give each team member time to reflect aloud on how they felt about the process, whether his or her voice was heard, whether he or she agrees with the outcome, and what he or she might have done differently. This activity should give your team some insight into the way the team makes decisions. Use this insight to create a plan for addressing real decisions.

Full-page version on page 147

- Be proactive about team consensus building and decision making. Don't wait until there is a crisis. Consider models that might work for the team.

- Get to know each individual team member's decision-making styles. Help team members learn each other's styles, comforts, and discomforts around decision making.

- Come up with a team process that honors these differences. Work together to make sure every decision the team makes is filtered through the question: Does this meet the needs of our students?

The importance of working out ways to make decisions and resolve conflicts cannot be overestimated. The process around making the decision will have longer-lasting effects than the decision itself.

Mentoring New Teachers

Being a first year teacher can be very overwhelming. I got lucky; my team was knowledgeable, positive, and always up for a good laugh. We had one common goal: to do what was best for kids. We all brought different perspectives to the table. This showed me that teams work best when they build from each other's strengths and ideas.

Brett Stern
Edwards Middle School
Brunswick, OH

Many educators leave the teaching profession after only three to seven years. The statistics show that in many cases this early exodus is due to teacher burnout: a feeling of being overwhelmed, lack of parental support for students, and issues with fellow educators. It is critical that we keep great middle level teachers. A team and the teaming process are perfect vehicles for nourishing and supporting new teachers.

New teachers provide us with a new perspective and a new outlook on kids, curriculum, and professional development. However, they can be very intimidated by the big circus we call elementary, middle, or high school. In some places, the middle school classroom can be an isolated space that is lonely and cold, very similar to the cages that keep circus animals penned up.

Middle schools need not only to provide quality mentors for new teachers, they also need to make sure that teams take care of the new hires.

Veteran teachers need to understand that many new teachers are often afraid to offer new ideas in the team meeting. Established teams might bulldoze a new teacher into accepting their way of doing things. When a team has a new hire, it is wise to share with the new teacher consistency practices that have been effective for the students and teachers on the team.

However, the team may want to also seek out new ideas and practices. Many new middle level teachers have some innovative and creative ideas that might just put a spark into a team and its team members.

It is important that new teachers meet with strong, experienced teachers on the team for advice and casual mentoring. New teachers need a team with whom they can share ideas and vent as necessary—a team who will not judge or make them feel inferior or silly.

> Let's be honest, your district may provide a teacher policy and procedural handbook; however, only a team member will tell which secretary not to talk to until she has had two cups of coffee, or better yet, where to find printer paper.

It is wise to have a new teacher spend a day watching her or his teammates teach. This will allow for the new teacher to see their students in other classrooms and to see the teaching styles used by other teachers on the team.

The truth is, new teachers will love the fact that a team has established team norms and rules. It will help them with consistency and provide them with structure. New teachers also need to understand that at times the middle school can be a little hectic. But that consistency helps keep *the circus* going.

Including Elective Teachers

Especially in large schools where elective teachers teach large numbers of students from multiple teams, effective teaming provides streamlined communication. Elective teachers can have a single contact person for each team through which information about students and team logistics and activities can flow. In many cases, elective teachers may see twice to three times as many students in one week than the regular team. Elective teachers can turn to effective teams when needing to address student concerns, because these teams have been possibly creating closer relationships with students.

On teams where elective teachers are a part of the teaming process, the elective teacher becomes a valuable member of the academic community, where core subject areas and elective content areas can work together for student success. Open communication provides an opportunity of cross-curricular instruction and a better understanding of adolescent development. In these effective teams, elective teachers understand the importance of choice elective classes for the developing child.

Shane Wuebben

In most schools with teaming, there is an onging question about what to do with elective teachers in the context of teams. (I like to refer to them as the "essentials teachers.") Here is a list of common questions regarding essentials teachers:

- Should they be their own team?

- Should they be on a team with the core teachers?

- Should they not be teamed at all?

- Should they just be allowed to do lunch duty and not deal with teams?

Chapter Eight

- How do we handle the shared essential teachers?

- Do essentials teachers want to be on a team?

Each of these questions is valid. Teachers and administrators ponder what is best for the teachers and the students. Let me say there is no single right answer. You have to decide what is best for your school, your teams, and your kids.

For example:

- Arcola Middle School has two teams. They have an Expressive Arts Team and a PE and Health Team. Both meet at separate times during the day. They focus on kids, curriculum, and professional development. They are aware that they never see all of the kids in the building, yet they look for ways to connect curriculum and deal with logistics.

- Meanwhile, at Perkins Local Middle School, they have a team of unified arts (essentials) teachers who all meet together. As a team they work on ways to support the core teams (helping to add phone calls that they make to the team's Google Docs™, asking teams to share any and all 3-5-3 plans with them). Have they perfected this line of communication? No! But they are constantly looking for ways to increase good communication between the electives and core teams.

Communication is one of the biggest issues with core and noncore teams. In many cases, core teams feel that they are keeping the essentials teachers in the loop. Yet, the essentials teachers always feel they are the last to know about things within the team. It is key that *every* team has a communicator who will inform the other teams of any interventions plans, and that essentials teachers work on keeping the core team informed of any student issues or concerns they are seeing in their classes.

Create a schedule that allows essentials teachers to meet and discuss logistics, kids, curriculum, and professional development. In many cases, the essentials teachers feel they are left behind with so much emphasis on core subjects. Recognizing their need to work with or as a team is the most professional thing to do.

We have abandoned some great essentials classes in this country, and we have not made the necessary changes to advance some of our essentials. We need to branch out and create new essentials that are innovative and creative. We need essentials teachers to realize that they are critical to the teaming process, and to do that, they need time to meet.

Essentials teachers have the responsibility to step up and spend time in their team meetings thinking about new curriculum and new classes that truly meet the needs of young adolescents. Why? The answer is simple: As my very good friend Kathy Hunt Ullock has always said, "The worst part of the apple for many kids is the *core*." With that said, we need to be reminded that for many of our young adolescents, *essentials* classes are what bring them to school.

Using Team Time Effectively

It is like herding cats!

J. Howard Johnson

The hardest part of taming a team is to keep everyone on task and focused during team meetings. Just as in the circus, a middle school team meeting can have several things going on at the same time. Teachers are coming and going at various times, there are endless interruptions, and at any moment the secretary might call someone about the last-period attendance sheet. If you don't have the taming down, a team meeting can turn into a three-ring circus—only without the organization of a real circus.

For those of us who are ADD, we can be easily distracted at the slightest movement or sparkly light. Yet, many teams refuse to set up an agenda. Here is the dilemma: Many educators feel that they are responsible professionals who can stay on task. However, that is not true. Teachers "birdwalk" with the best and can be pushed off task by the slightest mention of who got voted off of a reality TV show. We need something to keep us on task. Time is the most important issue for educators, and we are tired of our time being wasted.

Making Commitments about Team Meetings

Early on in your life together as a team, have a discussion about the reasons for a group of teachers to meet together. Ask each other: "Why do we come together?" During this discussion, everyone provides a reason for the team to meet. You might get answers such as:

- Talk about kids
- Discuss curriculum
- Work on professional development goals

Chapter Nine

- Vent and be around semimature adults
- Work on logistics
- Talk about team norms and expectations
- Meet with parents and students
- Work on the weekly homework calendar
- Update the team website
- Review student data and progress

The list will be varied and can be long. But awareness of and agreement on your purposes for meeting will become a basis for planning your meetings.

Also, ask and discuss questions such as:

- How often will we meet?
- What is the start and end time for our meetings?
- How will the agenda be established?
- How shall we begin and end each meeting?
- How can we assure that everyone feels safe to express opinions?
- What are the nonnegotiables that will make meetings run smoothly?
- What should we expect from each team member in terms of participation and engagement?
- How do we hold each team member accountable?

And most importantly:

- What do we want to be sure happens at each meeting (or every few meetings)?

Agree on answers to these questions. Agree on some expectations about the purpose and the norms for team meetings.

Setting an Agenda

Once you have agreed on what is important to do at your meetings and how each member will participate and be committed to the team process, you're ready for regular planning.

A team meeting is not about putting on your Birkenstocks and sitting in a circle singing "Kumbaya"! We need something to keep us on task. Time is a hot issue for educators, and we are tired of our time being wasted. *A team meeting should never be a waste of time.* Therefore, take a few minutes at the beginning of each meeting to create an agenda. You will already have agreed on how your agenda will be established, how meetings will be run, and what important things to cover.

Be sure that your agenda focuses on kids, curriculum, professional development, some fellowship, logistics, and other business. Be careful not to let "housekeeping" details take up too much of the time. Make the agenda fit the needs of your team. This should come easily because you began your teamwork together by discussing, "Why do we come together?"

Dealing with Different Personalities

One of the main reasons to create a great team agenda is to make sure to keep the *lions* (aka *teachers*) on task. In addition to coping with interruptions and crazy schedules, every team must also deal with the different personalities of its members. Do you recognize any of these teachers?

The Bulldozer

This person will plow right over others. They never have time to talk and can take over a meeting in a heartbeat. They always look busy, but rarely are. They often are afraid of being placed on a schoolwide committee. The Bulldozer is good at dealing with issues and making sure a task gets completed.

The Nurturer

Nurturers feel that "eating makes a meeting." When things get difficult, they make cupcakes and the world is a better place. They avoid conflict, yet are often involved in it in some way or another. They have been known to start off a conversation by saying, "Don't tell her I said this, but . . . ." Their hearts are in the right place, but they sometimes go overboard or often overreact. Nurturers are experts at dealing with parents and students.

The Spastic Teacher

I am very much like this teacher. I can soar, but I have no landing gears. The spastic teacher is the one who unloads twenty other people from the clown car, but has no idea how the clowns got into the car. This teacher might say things like, "I am going to turn the room into the space shuttle," but has no plan to make the transformation happen. Spastic teachers have the best intentions, but lack the follow through and focus. The spastic teacher will do anything that is asked, but is really focused on kids. Do not put them in charge of ordering the bus for the field trip.

Miss Dazed and Confused Teacher

I love this teacher! Miss Dazed and Confused walks around asking if today is the field trip. She thinks the meeting is in the library, even though everyone else is in the cafeteria. She asks the same question that was just asked and sometimes lacks focus and vision. (*Please note: Mr. Dazed and Confused can be found on any school staff as well.*) Both are fun to be around and will make you laugh, and they will do anything for anybody. They just can't find their car keys.

Every one of these teachers (and all the others that you might find on your team) probably have a different idea of how to run the team meeting. The best way to keep everyone on task is to create the best agenda possible. Agendas help teams stay on task and serve as a valuable record of the meetings. Decide what components are essential for your team agenda.

Exemplary teams recommend that at the end of a meeting a team should be able to review the agenda and see:

- When did the meeting take place?
- Who was there?
- What was discussed?
- What was decided?
- Who is responsible for implementation or the next steps?
- When should implementation be completed?
- When will each item be revisited?
- What should go on an upcoming agenda?

Review these sample team-meeting agenda formats as a starting point for developing your own template.

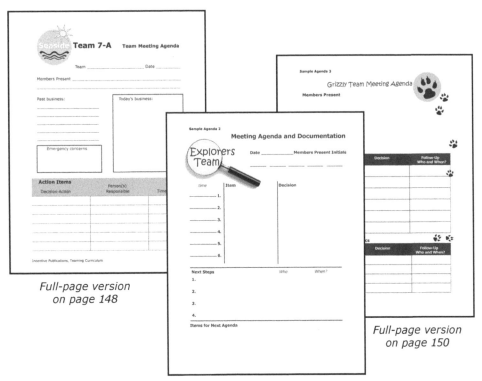

*Full-page version
on page 148*

*Full-page version
on page 149*

*Full-page version
on page 150*

Collecting Student Information

*Organizing is what you do before you do something, so
that when you do it, it is not all mixed up.*

A.A. Milne

Today, educators usually have several different grade book
programs that schools and school districts have purchased
for hundreds of thousands of dollars. These programs help
to collect academic data. The programs are helpful to parents
and students. They also allow teachers to enter grades and
help everyone access lists of students who are missing work
and assignments.

Yet, there are still individual teachers on a team who keep
a separate phone log when they call parents. Many team
members are keeping separate notes on team meetings,
separate lists for student of the week, or meetings with
parents and students. This can be very disorganized and
create a problem when a parent or administrator asks about
individual student information.

In reality, teachers in teams need to have *one place* to gather
and access all student information that is not related to grades
and missing assignments. Great teams have a central location
and system for keeping track of their students. For example, in
years past, teams in Perkins School District started collecting
data on students and placing the information in a file folder.
They created a file folder for each student. They loved the idea
of being able to look at a student's file folder and see how many
times teachers might have made positive or negative phone
calls home. They were also able to see if the student had been
brought into a team meeting. They could access how many

times the parents had attended conferences in the course of the year.

Each student file folder included:
- Parent contact information—phone, address, and e-mail
- E-mails that had been sent to teachers or to the team
- Samples of student work
- Discipline referrals
- Notes from meetings or phone calls with parents; copies of e-mails to and from parents
- Notes from student meetings
- Sample 3-5-3 (See page 75 for more on 3-5-3 plans.)
- Any other information important to the team about the student

The folder allowed team members to see all communications that had occurred over the course of the year between school, teacher, parent, and student.

The hardest part of this (or any centralized system) turned out to be maintenance of the files. To solve this problem, the team created a Google Doc™ for each student. Google Docs™ is a free, web-based office suite and data storage service offered by Google™. It allows users to create and change documents online in collaboration with other users. Everyone on the team could contribute to and update the same document. The team loved this easy way to maintain and access the student information.

If you use Google Docs™, make sure you create a template prior to creating the electronic file for each student. This will solve the problem of going back and creating a new document for each student. Here are some advantages of using a Google Doc™.

- Easy to use
- Allows all teachers to access information if they are invited by the team to access student information

- Multiple teachers can work on a student file at the same time

- All information is in one location

- Administrators can access all student files

- Helps teachers see how many times students' parents have been contacted and for what reasons

Be aware that when using Google Docs™, there are some issues to consider. First of all, remember that there are other systems out there. Google Docs™, is just one choice. You may need to talk with your IT director regarding the use of a system that is not attached to the district server.

You also need to make sure that when you create the template for the Google Doc™ it has all the elements and sections you need. It is not easy to add sections once you duplicate the template.

Decide who should contribute to and have access to the Google Doc™. Feel free to add an administrator, counselor, and the essentials teachers. However, the fewer people involved the better. This document will have student information and data, so be thoughtful about how many people have access to it.

Standard information you will want to collect:

- Student name
- Contact information
- E-mail information
- Phone information
- Date of any contact, type of contact, who made the contact, outcome
- Rewards and interventions
- 3-5-3 plans
- Other information that relates to your school or team

The overall goal of both the student file folder system or the Google Docs™ program is to have one central location for student contact and information. It is crazy for every teacher on a team to keep a different record. In order to help influence change, teams need to collect all information in one place. Teachers, teams, and administrators really want to see a complete picture of a student. It is important to be able to provide accurate data when dealing with a student.

Files like these are like a student personal data file—they contain all vital information for each student. The files become the script the ringmaster uses to make sure everything is organized for the greatest show on earth—a blueprint that helps you build a comprehensive plan for your student. And in the worst-case scenario, it can be used for a student expulsion hearing or court case.

Note: Whether the gathering place for student information is a file folder or a computer document, it must be easily accessible by the whole team. Make sure that team members understand that these records are private and need to be handled according to all the rules of the school and state and federal government regarding student privacy and confidentiality.

Creating a Team Discipline Process

The best people to deal with discipline are the classroom teachers and teams—not the administrator!

Jack Berckemeyer

Lines of Defense!

Here is the best truth I know about classroom discipline: If you throw a kid out of your class 30 times, they come back 31. Unless you win the teacher lottery, which is home schooling!

There are five lines of defense regarding classroom management. The first line is always the teacher; the second is the parent; the third is the team; fourth, the counselor; and last is the administrator. In most cases, teachers skip steps two through four and go directly to five.

We often ask administrators to step in and help us deal with classroom management issues before we need to. Be honest: They have little or no relationship with the student and they usually have very little background on a situation (other than a lengthy referral that was written in haste and anger by the classroom teacher). Administrators can tell that a teacher is mad by the number of exclamation points and the torn spot on the referral note where the words are underlined nine times.

If teams use their own discipline process to take care of classroom management issues, student behaviors will change. However, this process takes time and energy. Before teams can administer consequences to their students, there is a fine sense of balance that needs to be created between the team and administrators. Teachers can't have the power to suspend kids anytime they feel like it. I was so angry once, I would have suspended a kid for eight weeks, when there were only four weeks of school left!

Teams need to set up a process to deal with students and their behaviors. They need to create a discipline plan and discuss it with their administrators.

> *Our discipline process is a rewarding and powerful tool that helps us maintain discipline within our team. There is something to be said about taking control over a discipline situation right now, instead of passing it off to administration and then not always knowing the outcome. Having control of discipline provides instant feedback to students and allows our team to continue to monitor and work with them to make sure they get back on track.*
>
> *Jess Van Ness • Ali Lange*
> *Briar Middle School*
> *Sandusky, Ohio*

Every team should address the following classroom discipline problems as a team and should be ready, as a team, to deal with related student problems.

1. Tardies

2. Late work

3. No materials

4. Minor disruptions

5. Off-task behavior

6. No motivation

7. Minor arguments with other students

8. Running, pushing, and other adolescent behaviors

Teams should not deal with these discipline problems:

1. Drugs

2. Weapons

3. Fighting

4. Harm to a teacher or another student

5. Extreme language issues

So many referrals are written in the heat of the moment and, in some cases, should never have been written. Having the team write a referral allows team members to talk about the situation. There is a lot of power in a team referral.

Developing a Discipline Plan with Your Team

Great teams create a plan (in advance) for dealing with discipline problems. They develop a solid discipline process and discuss it with their administrators. This allows for common protocols when it comes to dealing with students and their progression of negative behaviors. Creating and evaluating a comprehensive discipline process can stop traditional comments within your building—"I sent them to the office and they did nothing!"

Any team discipline process must include the following 10 elements—statement of issue, examples of issue, proactive interventions, strategies for changing behavior, documentation of student responses, consequences and rewards, planned follow-up, support from administration and counselors, last resort idea, and administrative team decision.

Discipline Process Form

Issue	Response
Start by choosing a discipline issue such as tardiness, late work, disrespect, or lack of materials	

Examples	Response
Create a list of behaviors or examples that align to the issue.	

Proactive Interventions	Response
This is where the actual discipline process starts! Ask team members would they would do if began having the problem at issue. For example, what if students began forgetting their materials? Team members think of ways to proactively deal with the issue. Examples: talk with student, provide materials, or even meet a student at his or her locker in the morning to make sure materials for the day are in hand. The goal here is to make sure the team is dealing with issue and trying to solve the problem before it becomes a bigger issue.	

Strategies	Response
Plan strategies to use if the proactive approaches are not working to change the behavior. (Reference Creating Strategies to Help Change Behavior in Chapter 12.)	

Responses and Documentation	Response
Teams must document the steps taken during the proactive interventions and development of strategies. Use a student file folder or Google Docs. In order to make sure you have a complete picture of the student, great teams make sure they have outstanding documentation.	

Full-page blank version on page 151

Discipline Process Form page 2

Consequences and Rewards	Response
Make sure that during the planning process, you are creating real and immediate consequences for students. These rewards must be realistic.	

Follow-up	Response
Great teams know that you must schedule several follow-up sessions with students. Include both one-on-one conversations and team follow-up sessions.	

Support	Response
During this entire process make sure your administrators or counselors are providing support to the team as they create the plan and create strategies. There is nothing more frustrating then sending a student to the office and then the administrators suggest five new ideas to deal with the students. Lack of communication creates aggravation and frustration for the both the team and the administrators. Great administrators spend time in team meetings helping the team create ideas, so if the team referral is necessary the administrators know the team has done everything in their power to change the student behavior.	

Last Resort Idea	Response
In the movie "Saving Private Ryan" The character played by Tom Hanks says, "If all else fails, blow up the bridge." Every team needs to have a last resort idea. This idea is used after all else has failed. It is done when the team and the student have nothing else to loose in the process.	

Administrative Decision	Response
If the last resort has been tried and fails, then the case becomes the administrative team's issue. The administrators will do this with clear documentation of the steps that have already been taken and will involve the team in the creation of the new plan.)	

Full-page blank version on page 152

Build your discipline process on these 10 elements. Use the Discipline Process Form as a simple template.

Issue

Start by choosing a discipline issue such as tardiness, late work, disrespect, or lack of materials.

Examples

Create a list of behaviors or examples that align to the issue.

Proactive Interventions

This is where the actual discipline process starts!

Ask team members what they would do if they began having the problem at issue. For example, what if students began forgetting their materials? Team members think of ways to proactively deal with the issue. Examples: talk with student, provide materials, or even meet a student at his or her locker in the morning to make sure materials for the day are in hand.

The goal here is to make sure the team is dealing with an issue and trying to solve the problem before it becomes a bigger issue.

Strategies

Plan strategies to use if the proactive approaches are not working to change the behavior. (Reference *Creating Strategies to Help Change Behavior* in Chapter 12.)

Responses and Documentation

Teams must document the steps taken during the proactive interventions and development of strategies. Use a student file folder or Google Docs™. In order to make sure they have a complete picture of the student, great teams make sure they have outstanding documentation.

Consequences and Rewards

Make sure that during the planning process, you are creating real and immediate consequences for students. These rewards must be realistic.

Follow-up

Great teams know that you must schedule several follow-up sessions with students. Include both one-on-one conversations and team follow-up sessions.

Support

During this entire process make sure your administrators or counselors are providing support to the team as they create the plan and create strategies. There is nothing more frustrating than sending a student to the office only to have the administrators suggest five new ideas for dealing with the students. Lack of communication creates aggravation and frustration for both the team and the administrators. Great administrators spend time in team meetings helping the team create ideas, so if the team referral is necessary, the administrators know the team has done everything in their power to change the student behavior.

Last Resort Idea

In the movie *Saving Private Ryan*, the character played by Tom Hanks says, "If all else fails, blow up the bridge." Every team needs to have a last resort idea. This idea is used after all else has failed. It is done when the team and the student have nothing else to lose in the process.

Administrative Decision

If the last resort has been tried and has failed, then the case becomes the administrative team's issue. The administrators will then create a plan for the student. (Note: The administrators will do this with clear documentation of the steps that have already been taken and will involve the team in the creation of the new plan.)

Addressing a Discipline Issue in a Team Meeting

Before you deal with discipline in a team meeting where the student is present, plan ahead. Note: I have seen some really bad team meetings with students where teachers announce the 54 reasons they don't like the kid. Every teacher talks, repeating what others have said. The kid is beaten down so badly that the adult talk is tuned out.

1. That means that before you bring a kid into the meeting, as a team you must consider these questions:

    • What is the purpose of the talk with the student?

    • What is the desired outcome?

    • Will there be a follow-up, a phone call home, a meeting with the parent, an e-mail to the counselor, or will the student be asked to come back in a week for follow-up?

    • Who will do the talking? Never let everyone talk; it is unfair to the student. Never let everyone take a turn at saying something negative to the student.

2. Select one person on the team to talk. This is hard for us as classroom teachers to do; we all feel the need to talk. My friend Judith Baenen always told me that teachers constantly look for solutions and never really listen to the issues.

3. Outline the items to discuss with the student, keep them simple, and offer suggestions on how to change behaviors. The student's plan of action should include a list of issues, strategies that offer support, and ways to follow up with the student. (For more discussion on creating a Student Plan of Action, see Chapter 12.)

The meeting should take fewer than five minutes.

Using a 3-5-3 Action Plan

Planning without action is futile, action without planning is fatal.

Author Unknown

Creating Strategies to Help Change Behavior

Creating a successful action plan for a student may at first seem as daunting as training a cage full of lions. Yet, just as the lion tamer carefully teaches a sequence of behaviors that ultimately leads to the awesome final trick, the team must create a plan that leads to the student's success.

The 3-5-3 Action Plan—three core issues, five strategies for change, three ideas for follow-up—is an action plan with a purpose. The following paragraphs outline the development of a 3-5-3 plan. This step-by-step process helps teachers focus on a student's issues and concerns, as it provides a forum to discuss and pinpoint strategies that will ultimately change the issues.

Please note that the process includes not only the identification of issues and the development of strategies to change problems, but also planned follow-up ideas. The follow-up is the key to the success of a 3-5-3 plan. If teachers don't follow up with a student, then academic issues or behavioral concerns will never change.

How to Create a 3-5-3 Action Plan

Creating a 3-5-3 plan takes some time and dialogue. It is the team's chance to identify the issues and concerns surrounding a student's academic or behavioral issues.

1. **To start the process, create an inclusive, master list of the issues facing the student.** Separate the items on the list into two columns—one column for academic issues and one column for behavioral concerns.

   The team must create this list before talking with the student.

   > While creating this list, feel free to take some time to vent regarding the student's behaviors or lack of academic progress. It helps to dialogue about the problems students are facing. After the team has done several of these, they move along very quickly.

   An example of this first step:

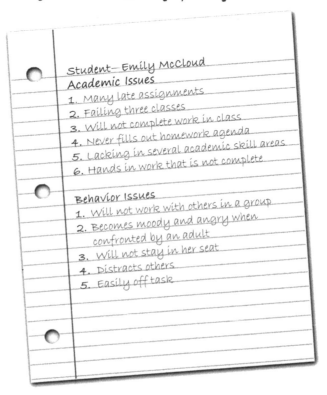

```
Student—Emily McCloud
Academic Issues
1. Many late assignments
2. Failing three classes
3. Will not complete work in class
4. Never fills out homework agenda
5. Lacking in several academic skill areas
6. Hands in work that is not complete

Behavior Issues
1. Will not work with others in a group
2. Becomes moody and angry when
   confronted by an adult
3. Will not stay in her seat
4. Distracts others
5. Easily off task
```

2. Choose three academic or three behavior issues as a focus. This is the first 3 in the 3-5-3 Action Plan.

It is apparent that Emily, in the example, has more than one issue. In fact, it might seem difficult at first to narrow down the list. However, as a team, you must choose no more than three academic issues or three behavior issues as a focus.

3-5-3 PLANNING FORM

Student name _____Emily McCloud_____ Date ___10-23___

3 **Issues:** Three Academic Issues
1. Not completing work in class
2. Missing assignments
3. No homework agenda

5 **Strategies for moving forward**
1.
2.
3.
4.
5.

3 **Ways to follow up**
1.
2.
3.

Student signature _____

Parent or guardian signature _____

Teacher signature _____

Full-page blank version on page 153

Taming of the Team

This is critical. When explaining an issue to the student, do not mix the two sides of the list. Focus on one or the other. Why? It is simple: The student is between 10 and 15 years old. Adolescents can't react or change behaviors when they hear a list of 45 reasons for things they need to change by tomorrow! If there are only two issues, don't add additional issues. Simply create a 2-5-3 plan.

3. Brainstorm a list of strategies that address the three core issues. This is the 5 in the 3-5-3 Action Plan.

Keep the selected focus issues in mind as the team develops a list of strategies for moving forward. Once the team has created a list of possibilities, choose the five to use in the action plan.

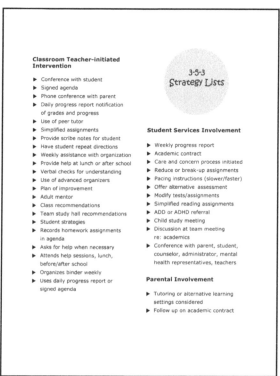

Full-page version on page 154

There need to be at least five strategies in the plan. Why? Great middle level teachers know that they may try 10 ideas before they finally get one that works. So, have at least five *realistic* strategies ready.

3-5-3 Planning Form

Student name ____Emily McCloud____ Date __10-23__

(3) Issues: Three Academic Issues

1. Not completing work in class

2. Missing assignments

3. No homework agenda

(5) Strategies for moving forward

1. At the end of each class period, Emily will fill out her student agenda and show it to her teacher.

2. Emily will remain in language arts class if she does not complete her work.

3. Emily will need to have her mom and dad sign the agenda book every Monday.

4. Emily with stay after class with Mr. Berckemeyer on Monday and Wednesday to finish her missing work.

5. For the next week Emily will receive some modified language arts assignments to help her catch up with her missing work.

(3) Ways to follow up

1.

2.

3.

Student signature _____

Parent or guardian signature _____

Teacher signature _____

Full-page blank version on page 153

In many cases, teachers struggle with creating these strategies. Teachers are great at coming up with a consequence in the heat of the argument with the student, but can struggle with creating a list off the top of their heads. *Let me clarify: Sending the student to Cuba for isolation purposes is not an example of a realistic strategy.*

Remember, this is a sample. You are creative! Come up with your own strategies. You know what works for your students!

4. Develop three ways to follow up and coach the student. This is the final 3 in the 3-5-3 Action Plan.

This last step in the 3-5-3 development process is the most important. It also takes the most amount of time. Once again, change happens when teachers make a concerted effort to provide follow-up and coaching for a student when they exhibit problem behaviors. The follow up can include rewards and a structure to monitor the student's progress.

Here is a simple list of follow-up ideas.

Please note: In the beginning there is no time or room for student input. The team identifies issues with the student and looks for ways to change behaviors. After a week of implementing the 3-5-3 plan, bring the

3-5-3
Follow-up
Ideas

▶ Student returns to team meeting in a week to make sure there has been some progress. This is critical and should be added to all 3-5-3 interventions.

▶ Call the parent.

▶ Notify the counselor.

▶ Create a self-monitoring check list for the student.

▶ Use of agenda book—check and verify that the agenda book is being completed.

▶ Notify principal.

▶ Add 3-5-3 to student folder.

▶ Seek student input after a couple weeks of activating the 3-5-3 plan.

Full-page version on page 155

student back into the team meeting. Have the student talk about what is working and what needs to be adjusted. But in the beginning, send a clear and consistent message that behaviors need to change.

I am a realistic person: Does this work with all students? NO! Will this program change your life, like the Ginsu Knife? NO! But it is one more strategy to help students get back on track.

3-5-3 PLANNING FORM

Student name ___Emily McCloud___ Date ___10-23___

(3) Issues: Three Academic Issues

1. Not completing work in class

2. Missing assignments

3. No homework agenda

(5) Strategies for moving forward

1. At the end of each class period, Emily will fill out her student agenda and show it to her teacher.

2. Emily will remain in language arts class if she does not complete her work.

3. Emily will need to have her mom and dad sign the agenda book every Monday.

4. Emily with stay after class with Mr. Berckemeyer on Monday and Wednesday to finish her missing work.

5. For the next week Emily will receive some modified language arts assignments to help her catch up with her missing work.

(3) Ways to follow up

1. Emily will come back to the team meeting in a week to discuss the plan. She will need to bring her signed agenda book.

2. Team will call and notify parents about the 3-5-3 plan.

3. Mr. Berckemeyer will stay after school two days next week to help Emily make up her work. He will also modify some of her assignments.

Student signature _____

Parent or guardian signature _____

Teacher signature _____

Full-page blank version on page 153

Why Not an RTI?

RTIs (Responses to Intervention) can be overwhelming and cumbersome. A 3-5-3 plan is one way to start the dialogue with your students and to help change behaviors. In addition, it provides some great documentation to show that the team is trying new strategies with students.

Looking at the Whole Student

As teams progress with the creation and implementation of 3-5-3 plans, encourage them to attend to the wide variety of factors and influences in the students' lives. Though creating a 3-5-3 plan is simple and straightforward, considering multiple elements that affect a student's ability to learn or behave is not so simple. This guide, "Looking at All the Elements That Affect Students," can be very helpful.

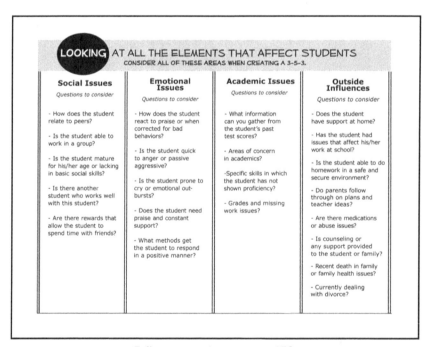

Full-page version on page 156

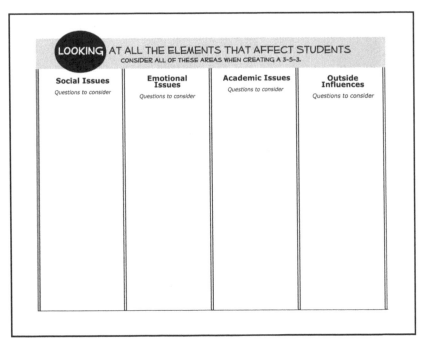

Full-page blank version on page 157

Teams can ask these questions as they work on 3-5-3 plans. Or they can use the blank template to gather their own items or questions in each category.

By answering the above questions and looking at the student in a holistic manner, you truly can paint a better picture of your student. This allows you to create new ideas and try new strategies.

Focusing on Kids

No significant learning occurs without a significant relationship.

Dr. James Comer,
Leave No Child Behind:
Preparing Today's Youth for Tomorrow's World

It is funny how we can mandate all kinds of curriculum, create revolutionary new standards, train educators to review and use data, and envision new programs while for too long, we have tolerated the bad teacher. We have defended the educator who can't say hello to a 13-year-old in the hall. We have even looked away when some teachers have skipped team meetings. Until we can make sure that middle grade teachers really enjoy being around young adolescents and really make them the center of the whole enterprise, we are spinning our wheels. This is why the Association for Middle Level Education emphasizes the importance of student advocacy and believes that having teachers who are committed to young adolescents is an essential part of the middle school model. Focusing on kids—really attending to their development and their needs and nurturing relationships with them—is not just about middle school. It should be the basic mission of all teams, at any level. This chapter is a call to action to all teachers, all teams, at all levels, to focus our vision, our goals, and our teamwork squarely on the students.

Maybe it is time for us to rise up and say, "Our school is about kids! This is our school; this is our team; and these are *our* kids!"

"But We Thought We Were Focused on Kids!"

Now, of course, just about every school insists that the students are the focus. It's even written in most schools' mission statements and in the vision or philosophy for most teams. We think we are focused on kids. We mean to be. Did you know that most teams spend the majority of their meeting time talking about kids? They do—as much as 60% or more.

> Yes, it is true that kids are our main focus, and in many cases they are easy to talk about—because they can be our common enemy. Therefore, it is easy to vent and discuss their latest escapades and antics. The problem comes when teams consume their time venting about the same student over and over again. Nothing changes.

There's the problem. All that time talking about kids is mostly venting. It's the tale-telling: "You'll never believe what Melissa did this week." It's commiserating about student behavior or parent noncooperation. It's lamenting the lack of consistency or responsibility or improvement. Furthermore, all that time is not even about *all* the kids; 95% of the time that teams *do* talk about kids, they are talking about just 5% of the student population.

And to deepen the problem, not nearly enough of the talking is about solutions. What teams need to be doing with their time are activities such as:

- Identifying the specific issues or behaviors that need to be addressed
- Agreeing on strategies to address specific issues
- Planning a way to redirect behavior for that kid
- Planning team-wide interventions
- Inviting a student to a team meeting to talk about concrete steps the student can take

- Agreeing how to combine all adult efforts to tackle a problem
- Giving a student a pep talk
- Meeting with parents to plan strategies for improvement
- Writing up a 3-5-3 Action Plan for a student
- Re-meeting with the student to see how the plan worked

If teams do that, they'll find that they can reduce the amount of time they spend talking in futility and use their time to set positive change in motion.

Often we think of ourselves as focused on our students, but we rarely talk about what that means, or check up on ourselves to see if we really are doing so.

What It Means to Be "Focused on Kids"

If you've read this far, you've heard me say more than once that the three major areas critical to teaming are—kids, curriculum, and professional development. So let's see how it looks for a team to be focused on kids. Then in the next few chapters, you'll get some idea of how it looks for a team to be focused on curriculum and professional development.

Here are 25 signs that a team has kids at the center of its vision, heart, and goals:

1. All team members get to know all the students.
2. The team members are very knowledgeable about the intellectual, social, emotional, moral, ethical, and physical *characteristics* of the developmental age of their students.
3. The team members are very knowledgeable about the intellectual, social, emotional, moral, ethical, and physical *needs* of the developmental age of their students.

4. The team has a vision statement soundly built on an understanding of the beliefs about students and committed to making happen what needs to happen for the students.

5. The team has a specific plan for how they will get to know each student well—academically, personally, emotionally.

6. Team members are committed to cultivating trusting relationships with students. The team identifies and practices specific strategies to do this.

7. Each team member knows something personal about each student.

8. Each team member greets each student on the team energetically and positively any time they meet.

9. You will often hear team members ask one another—in many situations—questions like this: "Is this good for the students?" "Will this further our goals for our students?" "Will this help the students become better learners?" "Will this increase academic success or social development or independence for students?" Everything passes through the "Is it good for kids?" filter!

10. Team members speak respectfully to and about the students.

11. Team members make concerted efforts to differentiate instruction so that students have chances to learn in ways best for them.

12. The team has clearly articulated academic expectations for students. Team members regularly help students to reach these expectations.

13. Student efforts and accomplishments are recognized regularly.

14. Students feel safe in their team environments—emotionally and physically.

15. Every student on the team is discussed at a team meeting at least twice during the year.

16. Students on a team will say they have a voice and many choices in all facets of classroom life and learning.

17. The team consciously plans ways for students to have input into classroom policies, procedures, problem solving, and learning experiences.

18. Students are asked for feedback on learning activities and classroom procedures.

19. Students are seen, heard, and valued.

20. Team members act to help students fit in and polish social skills.

21. Each team member communicates to students without ridicule, shame, sarcasm, or judgment.

22. All students' families and parents are considered to be an important part of the learning community. Team members cultivate positive, trusting relationships with parents.

23. Every student has one adult advocate assigned specifically to him or her.

24. Teams work together to build a list of ways to advocate for students. They share their advocacy ideas and experiences.

25. Teams plan celebrations to recognize and encourage all kinds of student accomplishments.

Building Significant Relationships

Note: You might be wondering why I waited until near the end of the book to talk about relationships. After all, without great relationships, nothing will ever work. If an administrator does not work well with his or her staff, no new programs will be developed. If teachers cannot get along and instead spend their time committing educational sabotage, then teacher morale will decline. If teachers cannot build strong, trusting relationships with students, then both teachers and students will struggle to succeed.

> Building relationships is not meant to be at the front or at the end of this book. It is meant to happen throughout the whole process of teaming. Everything that I have written in this book is ultimately about relationships.

Let's be honest—even the lion tamer has a relationship with the lions!

At the beginning of this chapter, there is a quote from James Comer. Note that he says, "No significant learning occurs . . . ." This applies to adults, too. The main point of this chapter about focusing on kids has its heart in both good advocacy and caring relationships. But the need for relationships goes beyond just relationships between teacher and student. One marvelous thing about teaming is the model the adults show to the students. A team of adults working together is a living model of relationships. It is a living model of learning and growth. Significant learning happens for us, too, in the presence of our significant relationships with our students and with other team members. If we don't work hard on building relationships with our students and with our teammates, three things are going to happen—I guarantee:

- Academic achievement will not rise.
- Teacher morale will decline.
- Young adolescents will have to navigate school without knowing they have caring adults watching their backs.

This may seem like an unusual goal—to actually start caring about students and being their advocate! After all, we are teachers. Aren't teachers all about kids? Well, that's what we like to think. But advocacy requires connection. And when a teacher sees 120 students a day—it becomes a lofty goal to make connections with every student.

There are many ways to make sure we are connecting with our kids. There are even ways to encourage the most reluctant teachers to build relationships with their students. This is a topic for your team meetings and for your team's professional development. I'll leave you here with one great way to set the stage for developing relationships with your students and for setting an advocacy system in motion.

This is called the Index Card Activity. It can be done any time after the first five weeks of school. This matches students with advocates on your team. Then it allows teachers to target students for whom they will advocate and commits to a policy that every child will have daily communication with an adult. (It is not about an advisory group or a homeroom. In many cases, students are in those classes because a computer selected them. This is a system where real live teachers choose to connect with students.)

The Index Card Activity

This activity could be done by an individual teacher, but it is more effective when done by a team.

Step One

Write every kid's name on an index card. If you have 120 kids on your team, then you should have 120 index cards. Please put both the students' first and last names on the index card. Write big so everyone can see the name on the cards.

Step Two

Place all the cards on the table, face up, with every name visible.

Step Three

Have the most experienced teacher on the team choose one student by picking up the index card. Teachers should pick a student whom they have come to know; a student who might make them smile; or the student who might make them crazy (but that would make the drive to the insane asylum fun).

Step Four

Once you pick the card, you must explain to the team why you picked that child. Just give a couple of examples.

Step Five

Have the next most experienced teacher pick a student and explain why. Repeat this three times for each team member.

Step Six

Complete several speed rounds—each teacher picks three names per turn (three or four rounds). Team members do not need to explain why they picked each kid, unless they want to.

Step Seven

Once there are about 20 names left on the table, stop and have everyone on the team look at the names. Ask, "Why has each of these students not been selected? Is it because no one on the team knows the student? Or is it because no one on the team likes the student? Or is it because the student is a behavior problem?"

Step Eight

Team members make sure every child is picked. You may have to trade two Bernices for a Bob and a better pick next year. Remember the goal is to have every child picked by a teacher. Once you have your set of cards, rotate five to seven of those cards every week. Make sure you make natural connections with those five to seven students. Check up on them, ask them how they are doing, talk about the weather or sports. Kids need to know someone cares.

Please note: Don't stop talking to other kids—you will still be talking to them as well.

Here are some hints for making this strategy work.

- After several weeks, you may need to trade a student to another teacher. A natural connection might not happen for you, but it will for another teacher.

- When picking the last 20 kids, teachers may not end up with exactly the same number of students. It is not about quantity, it is about quality.

- As a team, reflect on the 20 students that were not picked in the first several rounds and really ask each other why.

  Recently, I had a team take part in this activity, and they noticed that all of their special education students were left or not picked. They realized that as a team, they had a bias against these students. They proceeded to figure out why and correct that situation.

- After a while you can also use those index cards to form team groups and maybe even change your homeroom at semester break. Just a thought.

  While working in a school in Pennsylvania, I had a teacher who was a little reluctant to do the Index Card Activity. I asked him as a favor to please participate, and he did. When the 20 cards were left, he got really quiet and seemed upset. When I asked him why, he replied, "What if my child was one of those students left on the table?" This was an eye-opening experience for everyone. It made it real. These are real kids who need someone to care for them and watch out for them.

This index card strategy may seem simple, but it creates a touchstone and a tangible reminder to make sure we are connecting with our students.

Focusing on Curriculum

Teaming has allowed us to shift from isolated classroom to collaborative discussions centered on the curriculum needs of our students. Our teachers no longer feel alone as they try to meet the ever-changing standards. Now we can tackle them together with one common goal— student success.

Suzette Johnson
Hayden Middle School

A powerful team will break down fragmentation among subjects and interrelate the content of subjects taught by team members.

John Lounsbury

Student success—isn't that what we're all about? It *is* our goal. And we are so much more likely to reach that goal for all the students when we work well together in teams. The problem is that for many (maybe even most) teams, top-quality learning and student achievement are not the subjects that consume most of the time we spend together. As I mentioned in the last chapter, a huge amount of time is spent talking about kids—and most of that time, about only a few kids (and most of that time, not even finding solutions)!

As Rick DuFour wrote in a *2004 Educational Leadership* article, "Communication is the heart of collegiality." Yet, too much of team time is spent on the easy conversations such as, "Why did Johnny run into the wall four times?" and "What is up with the new schedule for Friday's Activity Day?" Teams need to get to the real conversations. And if our goal is to increase student success, we need to be talking (a lot) about curriculum and instruction. With the switch to Common Core State Standards moving into high gear across the nation, when will teachers really have time to talk about what the standards mean, how the teaching will be affected, what will be different for students, and how they will adapt to actually put them into practice? The answer is simple—during team time!

Changing the Way We Spend Our Team Time

If across the team and school, we spend the greatest percentage of our time talking about just a few kids (and mostly talking, not even finding real solutions), two outcomes will occur:

1. Academic achievement will not rise.

2. Teacher morale will decrease.

This is why great teams spend at least 25% of their team time on curriculum. A growing body of research is supporting what strong teams have "certified" casually in classrooms for years. When teams work together with a focus on improving learning for all students, student achievement rises. And the more time the adults plan, discuss, and grow together, the greater are the gains in student performance.

Making Connections Across the Disciplines

To address curriculum that affects all the students and teachers, teams need to be talking about their plans related to curriculum. All team members need to know what other team members are planning: what topics, themes, standards, and concepts will be covered; what kinds of activities will be offered; what teaching strategies will be used; what the expectations for students are; what the homework will be; what assessments are planned; what materials will be used; and what special events will be included. And team members need to know how all this fits into the calendar. So teams must make connections in curriculum, instruction, and the calendar. Here is a way to make those connections:

- During team meeting, have all teachers give an overview of what they will be teaching in the next week.

This should include:
  – Topics, themes, big ideas to be taught
  – Homework load and schedule
  – Project expectations for students
  – Tests and quizzes
  – Teaching strategies and types of learning activities planned
  – Standards to cover
  – Special events (such as field trips or presentations)

- When sharing your curriculum and instruction plans with the team, provide other team members with any vocabulary or spelling lists students will get for the week.

- Provide all team members a copy of any tests or quizzes you plan to give, along with the study guide you have given students.

- Share with your team reading assignments, stories, and challenge math problems your students will be expected to complete.

- Talk through the learning activities you have planned.

- Keep a team calendar for the week, showing what is being taught and expected of students. Post this on the team website.

- Fill out a student planner that is similar to the planner used by the students. Make sure it has each teacher's homework listed on the correct date.

- Step back and pause to look at the week's plans from each teacher.

- Look for places where curriculum can be aligned—where one concept or skill can be strengthened across all disciplines. Talk about how you can enhance this connection. Look for ways to parallel teach a concept.

- Look for ways that you can modify an assignment or project to connect it to something another teacher is teaching. Ask each other for examples and ideas.

- Talk about the activities you each intend to use. Rearrange or change these to complement the other experiences students will have in other subject areas. (For example, if you see that all four or five of you planned to build a clay model of something—a few of you might want to switch your plans!)

- Talk about instructional strategies. Try to arrange the days so that students have a healthy variety of learning adventures.

- Once a month, have a team member share a teaching strategy that has worked well to engage students.

- Talk about the standards you plan to cover. Perhaps try to touch on or focus on the same standard across all disciplines. Discuss ways you can deepen that standard with joint efforts.

- Use forms to set goals for making curriculum connections. Note the three sections.

    – Under Curriculum Connections, set a few goals for ways you will make connections by addressing common themes, topics, concepts, or standards.

Full-page version on page 158

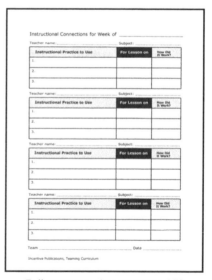

Full-page version on page 159

– Under Instructional Connections, set goals for kinds of instructional practices you will use.

– After reviewing the calendar, use the Calendar Connections page to make adjustments and commitments about what team efforts you will make to coordinate items on the calendar.

• See pages 161–162, *Ways to Connect Curriculum,* for more suggestions about ways to connect curriculum.

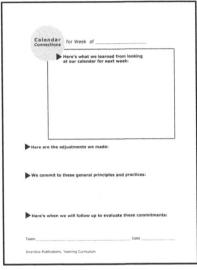

Full-page version on page 160

Full-page version on page 161

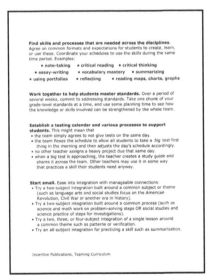

Full-page version on page 162

When you have the weekly process down,

• Be adventuresome and map out a whole month. Place the curriculum for each subject area on the wall and see what topics overlap. In many cases, we re-teach a topic over and over again, or do the same basic activity over and over again—and then we wonder why our students are bored.

That is why when I am Ruler of Education, children won't graph types of candies after third grade.

- Take a few minutes each quarter to talk about the data trends related to your students. For example, if you know your students are not doing well with fractions, spend time as a team learning how to use fractions skills in all classes. This may be a struggle for some teachers who do not feel proficient in math or fractions. However, it can be done just by using common language. "Hey, class. We just read a short story that had two characters in conflict for half of the story and two more characters in conflict for another third of the story. What fraction of the story did not include any conflict among these characters?"

- As a team, start thinking about creating an interdisciplinary unit to be taught across the disciplines. See Chapter 15 for help with this.

Addressing Standards Together

Across the nation, most school districts are making a change to curriculum aligned with Common Core State Standards. For many teachers and students, the Common Core standards set a new paradigm for learning processes. These are not just a new set of higher standards—they are the first standards to focus on *how* students learn, not just on *what* they learn. There are new approaches and processes for instructional and planning processes. This is something that must be tackled within your team. In addition to whatever training your school or district gives, work on these together. Make sure all of you understand the standards that affect each other.

1. Get to know the Anchor Standards. Discuss how these can be supported by curriculum across the team.

2. Review all the literacy and math standards together. Make sure all team members understand how these are organized and how they are different from previous standards.

3. Become fluent in the English-Language Arts standards (beginning at Grade 6) for history and social studies, science, and technology.

4. Work to make lessons and activities that are engaging, fun, and incorporate the focus on evidence, analysis, problem solving, and deep understanding. Help each other find ideas for doing this within each subject area.

5. Develop sample questions to use across curricular areas that get students to real understanding of processes.

6. Fortify students' knowledge base and use it as a base to increase their understanding of increasingly complex concepts.

7. Together, lose your fear of the change. Take a proactive approach to use the new standards in the way they were intended: to fully prepare students for success in life, college, and the workplace. Use team time to discuss this topic. The more it is discussed, the easier it becomes. The more we share, the easier it is to implement. The more we argue and dig our feet in, the harder it becomes for us and for our students. We may all teach different topics, but if we're connected to each other and each other's curriculum, we can make it more meaningful and relevant in every class.

 Here is the deal—students see connections in curriculum. Teachers do not! The reason is simple: Students go from class to class. Teachers stay in one room—never experiencing the true connections that occur between classrooms and subject matter.

One sure way to increase achievement of students on your team is to start talking more about each other's curriculum. Teachers can skill, drill, and kill two weeks prior to the test, and scores will still not go up. Scores will increase when teams spend some of team time on curriculum concerns.

Creating Interdisciplinary Units

There is no need to use the shield of standards as an excuse not to be creative.

Rick Wormeli

In many cases, this is just what we have done. We have been bogged down by requirements and standards—and we have (often isolated from our colleagues) focused in with single-mindedness on benchmarks. In the process, we have lost or diluted emphases on many great educational concepts or goals. One of the most beneficial of those concepts (most effective in raising student achievement and energizing teachers) is connecting curriculum across the disciplines. Teaming is the natural setting for dynamic curriculum connections. And guess what? It's also a great way to really solidify and deepen the understandings articulated in the standards, too!

One of the best teaching practices for students is to parallel teach. That means teaching a concept in a specific subject area while another teacher teaches the same or a similar topic in their classroom. Students want to see natural connections, and when they do, learning becomes easier and more efficient. When teachers parallel teach a topic, it leads to a natural connection, and thus a true interdisciplinary unit is developed.

During the 1980's, it seemed that teams all over the country were developing units that did not have a natural curriculum connection, they were just fun. It was all about the culminating activity at the end. It was about building something and then letting students destroy it. In the course of my career, I have seen some of the worst units based on the Olympic games. Bobbing for apples is not the same as bobsledding.

Taming of the Team

In many cases, the best units:

- Are based on student interests and the curriculum
- Are short in duration (less than two weeks)
- Allow students to use prior knowledge and seek answers to their questions
- Do not force connections

> Time and time again, interdisciplinary units had to have math so the students were required to do a graph or a chart. "If it does not fit, do not make it fit!" We have all seen a pair of shoes we liked, but they were a size too small. In spite of that, we tried them on and we thought, "Oh, my feet are just swollen, they will fit better later." They don't fit and never will; let it go.

The hard parts about creating a successful interdisciplinary unit are the time the planning takes and the details that must be considered. Here are some thoughts to keep in mind as you move through the process:

1. Make sure you have a realistic topic that is highly motivating to young adolescents.
2. Units do not need all subject areas in the curriculum. Some of the best units are two-subject based.
3. Seek connections from essential and elective teachers.
4. Make sure the unit has identifiable outcomes for students.
5. Create a list of tasks for all teachers and students.
6. Think of how to use technology in the unit.

Curriculum Wheels

The curriculum wheel is a great tool for teams to use for planning an interdisciplinary unit. It provides a visual model of the unit—showing lessons, aspects, topics, or approaches to be covered by various members of the team.

The center of the wheel shows the theme or topic of the unit. Then, each of the spokes or wedges is assigned to one of the disciplines. The wheel has enough sections to include the elective or exploratory courses that students take. Each section is a place to write a summary of the skills, standards, topics or processes to be covered within that discipline or elective. Teachers can also add to the wheel categories that show what to do in advisory sessions, to encourage parent involvement, or to identify group field trips in support of the unit.

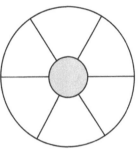

Full-page version on page 163

There may be times that an interdisciplinary unit is focused on a topic of interest to students. Other times, its purpose may be to enhance or extend understanding of a big idea. Don't miss opportunities also to build a unit that hones in on a specific process, standard, or skill that students need to master.

Here are some ideas of different kinds of units to plan.

An Interdisciplinary Unit Developed Around a Topic
For example:

- Space
- Mysteries
- Storms
- Ecology
- The Ocean
- Energy
- Volcanoes
- Poetry
- Environmental Change
- The Renaissance
- The Roaring Twenties

An Interdisciplinary Unit Developed Around a Big Idea
For example:

- Change
- Conflict
- Cycle
- Authority
- Movement
- Structure
- Transitions
- Relationships
- Cause and Effect
- Form and Function
- Effects of Technology
- Interdependence

An Interdisciplinary Unit Developed Around a Skill or Process
For example:

- Problem Solving
- Essay Writing
- Argument
- Inquiry
- Outlining
- Critical Reading
- Note Taking
- Speaking
- Analysis
- Evaluation
- Finding Evidence (Inquiry)
- Reading and Interpreting Visual Information
- Using Technology

An Interdisciplinary Unit Developed Around a Standard
For example:

An interdisciplinary unit can be used creatively to cover just about any of the Common Core State Standards—particularly in literacy—which applies to all subject areas.

See examples of curriculum wheels on pages 106–108.

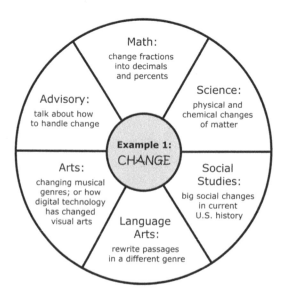

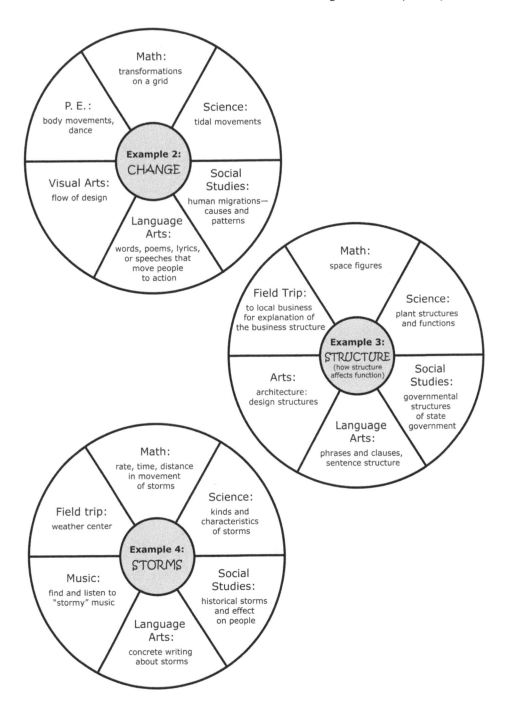

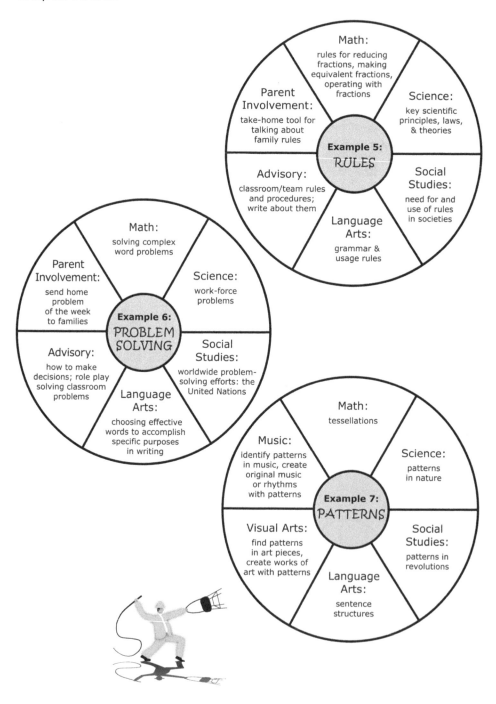

Example 5: RULES

Math: rules for reducing fractions, making equivalent fractions, operating with fractions

Science: key scientific principles, laws, & theories

Social Studies: need for and use of rules in societies

Language Arts: grammar & usage rules

Advisory: classroom/team rules and procedures; write about them

Parent Involvement: take-home tool for talking about family rules

Example 6: PROBLEM SOLVING

Math: solving complex word problems

Science: work-force problems

Social Studies: worldwide problem-solving efforts: the United Nations

Language Arts: choosing effective words to accomplish specific purposes in writing

Advisory: how to make decisions; role play solving classroom problems

Parent Involvement: send home problem of the week to families

Example 7: PATTERNS

Math: tessellations

Science: patterns in nature

Social Studies: patterns in revolutions

Language Arts: sentence structures

Visual Arts: find patterns in art pieces, create works of art with patterns

Music: identify patterns in music, create original music or rhythms with patterns

Taking a Flexible Approach to Scheduling

Flexible scheduling allows schools to optimize time, space, staff, and facilities and to add variety to their curriculum offerings and teaching strategies.

Robert Lynn Canady and Michael D. Rettig

The best practices in curriculum at the middle and high school levels are often hindered by the school schedule. To effectively deliver curriculum—particularly curriculum that involves connections across disciplines—we need time configurations that are not the "norm" for this level. To pull off an interdisciplinary unit, to really support authentic project-based learning, or to conduct a nonrushed science lab or other experimental hands-on learning situation, we need to have the kind of schedule that gives us bigger blocks of time. How else can we provide these critical, authentic learning experiences? This is why lots of good middle schools (and yes, even some high schools!) have moved to flexible scheduling.

One of the hardest elements to master on a team is flexible scheduling. Most teams and schools are tied to traditional class periods. That means classes last for 45-60 minutes. A few schools have embraced a block schedule within their school building, which allows for longer class periods and therefore provides some flexibility. However, most schools and districts that start using a block schedule never really spend time providing quality professional development about how to use this flexibility effectively. Teachers still tend to teach the same way. They just make sure the lesson lasts a little longer, or they give students more time to work at the end of their instruction.

Taming of the Team

If a school staff really wants to embrace the flexibility of a block schedule, they should look at a modified block. This schedule allows additional time for a given subject on some days and still allows for some days with standard 50-minute classes. Below is a simple example of a modified block.

Period	Monday	Tuesday	Wednesday	Thursday	Friday
1	Math 50 minutes	Math/ Science Block	Math 50 minutes	Math/ Science Block	Team Time
2	Science 50 Minutes	Math/ Science Block	Science 50 minutes	Math/ Science Block	Help and Support
3	Reading/ L.A. 50 Minutes	Reading/ L.A./Social Studies Block	Reading/ L.A. 50 minutes	Reading/ L.A. Block	Novel
4	Social Studies 50 Minutes	Reading/ L.A./Social Studies Block	Social Studies 50 minutes	Reading/ L.A. Block	Enrichment
5	Special or Essentials Classes	Essentials Classes	Essentials Classes	Essentials Classes	Essentials Classes
6	Special or Essentials Classes	Essentials Classes	Essentials Classes	Essentials Classes	Essentials Classes

- *Note: Essentials Classes are most commonly referred to as Electives or Specials.*

Our fear of embracing a flexible schedule has nothing to do with creativity or willingness to change. It has everything to do with a computerized schedule that must be printed. This printed schedule keeps us organized and allows the office to find a student when a parent comes to pick up a child for a brace tightening at the orthodontist.

> *Great teams that are willing to tame the status quo create several schedules for their students based on student and teacher needs, not the need of a*

computer program. For example, when I was on a team, students had three different schedules in their notebooks. We referred to the schedules as colors—we had a red day, which was their traditional computer printed schedule that was given to them at the beginning of the year. We had a blue day that allowed us to have block time. Then we had a yellow schedule that basically allowed us to have more time with students for major projects or hands-on lessons. It allowed my teammates to do more things like blow things up and really work on a specific task.

Here is an example of a Yellow Day Schedule (four class periods).

Monday	Tuesday	Wednesday	Thursday	Friday
Reading-Novel	Reading-Novel	Reading-Novel	Enrichment	Enrichment
Project time	Project time	Project time	Math and Science Lab	Presentations
Project time	Project time	Project time	Language Arts and Social Studies Lab	Presentations
Project time	Project time	Project time	Project time	Celebrations

In the above example, the team is able to move kids around, create new schedules, separate students who need to be separated, and give teachers more time to work on a team project or interdisciplinary unit. Students would go to their elective classes for the remainder of the day. This schedule only works if teams are given a block of time.

If there are breaks such as lunch or planning times, you can still create a different schedule. Just think of teaching time with students as your time, not the office's time and definitely not as a computerized printout.

In the Yellow Day Schedule shown on the previous page, each teacher did have to teach a novel and be part of the project that integrated all subjects. It took a lot of work as a team, but the students loved the flexibility and many of them enjoyed staying with one teacher for most of the day to work on their lesson or project.

A schedule that keeps the same kids with the same teacher for a long period of time might have a negative effect on the teacher and the student. You might be tired of hearing the same student ask the same question all day. However, there are benefits to sustaining and maintaining a relationship with your students, and it helps with delivering instruction.

A flexible schedule allows teams to control their time. Wouldn't it be great if your principal said, "Here is your team time, here are the amounts of time that we must teach these subjects, now go create a schedule based on your kids and your team."

Maybe that is just a fantasy I have dreamed up, but if artists at the circus can walk on a tightrope above the crowd, we can create a better schedule for our students.

Focusing on Professional Development

Teams of teachers who gather with a common purpose to improve teaching and learning in their classrooms over time become a community of learners.

Rick and Rebecca DuFour

An effective team is one of the best models of a professional learning community that I know. Unfortunately, we don't think of ourselves, the adults on the team, as the learners—at least not often enough.

I have said it before, and I will say it again. The three major areas critical to teaming are kids, curriculum, and professional development. When I step into a school to work with teams, the teachers are not surprised to hear me talk about focus on kids or focus on curriculum. They expect this. But most teams have not thought about the work of their team including their own professional development. Most are not thinking of their cooperating staff unit as a professional development unit—with their own growth and development as a goal. So I will get on my soap box again: "Hey, everyone! A great team sees the team and everyone in it as an amazing resource for professional development!"

Yes, you will grow and develop and learn and teach better—just by being a part of an effective team. But your team will be so much more mature and effective IF you consciously plan for new learning experiences within your team.

Never Stop Learning

Commit to use a portion of your team time for activities that inform, stretch, deepen, and improve you as teachers. Give yourselves the luxury of actually seeking learning opportunities together. Teams that deliberately engage in learning with each other grow as persons and as professionals.

In the midst of your very busy lives and schedules, teams must find ways to stimulate learning for themselves. Here are a few guidelines:

Think short. You do not have to plan exhaustive seminars or long meetings. Break something into manageable pieces. Each person can take a piece of an article, read and digest it, and share three take-away points with other teammates.

Think ahead. Watch out for concerns and needs that could lend themselves to some professional development. For instance, if you have a challenging decision to make, investigate some decision-making models. If a new standard or mandate comes your way—put it on your professional development agenda and be ready to each bring one idea about implementing it to your next meeting. If a rough situation comes up over and over during your teaching—ask a teammate to videotape you. An analysis and problem-solving session about the issue can be a good professional development experience for the team.

Think group. Look around your team. Remember that each person on your team is a great resource for professional development. When members share strategies, ideas, insights, mistakes—every other person is enriched.

Think organization. Gather ideas for team professional development. Spend some time culling the ideas and identifying those you need most. Build these into a menu of things you will pursue. Make a timeline—scheduling topics once or twice a month for several months in advance. When you put something on the schedule, assign a person to facilitate an activity around that topic.

Think variety. There are dozens of ways to do this together. Think outside the box! Read chapters of a book together and discuss them. Watch part of a DVD. Find a great article on a hot, current topic, and get the main points from it. Have each team member share an idea or technique that is his or her greatest strength. Invite another teacher with a great idea to come and share. Take a field trip. Do a sample lesson. Try out a new teaching technique together. Take turns presenting one idea each in a different modality. Visit a great website together. Watch and discuss a webcast. Share a great blog discovered by a teammate. The possibilities go on.

Topics for Professional Development

Here are a few topics you might pursue. Add your own ideas to the menu. Don't forget to add topics from your own curriculum, specific problems you are having, and urgent needs that arise.

- Social networks
- Social websites
- Bullying
- Classroom management
- Student motivation
- Teacher morale
- Analyzing and using student data
- Homework
- How to teach decision-making skills
- How to teach critical thinking skills
- How to teach summarization skills
- How to teach critical reading skills
- How to teach problem-solving skills
- How to teach test-taking skills
- How to teach note-taking skills

Chapter Seventeen

- Helping kids handle peer group pressure
- How to teach behavior-responsibility skills
- Formative assessment
- Use of technology
- Academic vocabulary
- Understanding new standards
- Implementing new standards
- Closing the achievement gap
- Interesting, current article
- Integrating instruction
- Curriculum mapping
- Responding to student work
- Student reflections
- Grading consistency

- Group dynamics
- Conflict resolution
- Effective questioning techniques
- Student voice and choice
- Brain-based learning
- Collaborative learning for kids
- Use of digital software
- Use of computers, notebooks, pads
- Relating to parents
- Student-led conferences
- Best instructional practice
- Making learning more active
- Behavior contracts
- Team public relations
- Independent study
- Project-based learning

Evaluating Your Team

Lay all the cards on the table, don't speak with hidden messages, be direct, honest, kind, professional, friendly, and—for goodness sake—keep a positive attitude and a good sense of humor.

Melba Smithwick
Paul R. Haas Middle School
Corpus Christi, Texas

Great teams spend time evaluating their effectiveness. They ask the tough questions, they drive through "Uglyville" to get to "Great," and they spend time reflecting on their areas of strength and concern. By the way, this is professional growth and development! So use some of your team time for it!

How do you know if you need to make some changes? Here are some questions that might help you decide:

1. Do you spend 95% of your time on the same 5% of your kids?

2. Are you using terms such as *these kids* or *those kids*?

3. Have you ever thought of divorcing your teammates?

4. Does one person control your team time?

5. Do you tend to focus on one team member who is not being a team player?

6. Are there days you crave the feeling of being a teacher in a one-room schoolhouse?

If you answered *yes* to several of these questions, take a few minutes during your next team meeting and discuss how to make your team more effective.

Introduce the topic with a humorous survey like this one:

This tongue-in-cheek reflection can help you ask each other the tough questions. Sometimes humor helps take the edge off the tough questions and comments that we need to make.

Full-page version on page 164

Work together to answer these questions as honestly as possible. As you do, realize that your team is not alone in grappling with any of these issues. So don't approach any of these with shame or blame. Just doing this kind of activity together will help your team identify your strengths. It will help you see where and how you spend your team time. It will put focus on your team's growth and development. It will remind you about the good work your team must do—far beyond spending huge amounts of time talking about students (much of it unproductively, and much of it on just a few of the students). It will remind you that when teams do use their time that way, other important teamwork—academic achievement for all students, curriculum connections, teacher morale, and professional growth—doesn't have a prayer.

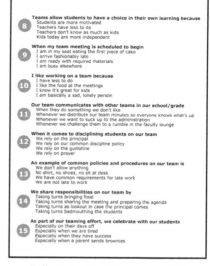

Full-page version on page 165

After you finish the reflection, don't drop it in a file and walk away. Identify items that are of concern—that need further discussion, a policy revision, more team time, or change. Put these on the agenda in future meetings as professional development work for your team. Complete the reflection again in several months, compare results, and celebrate improvements!

Research on teaming identifies attributes of effective teams. Great teams focus on these as a part of their structure and procedure. The professional development curriculum from Incentive Publications, *Elements of Effective Teaming*, is built around these elements:

- Team Philosophy and Vision
- Teamwork
- Team Meetings
- Consistent Team Protocols
- Student Voice and Choice

- Relationships and Student Advocacy
- Curriculum and Instruction Connections
- Team Communication with the School
- Team Communication with Parents and Families
- Team Professional Development

The rubric that follows is a sample of another way to evaluate your team's work and progress. It is built around the above 10 elements. Work together to agree where your team falls on each of these items. Again, don't shove this in a drawer after you finish. Make the results a part of your ongoing discussion. Identify some specific strategies to make improvement. Make the team's needs part of future professional development for the team. Complete the rubric again in several months and reflect on the results. Celebrate your team's growth in effectiveness!

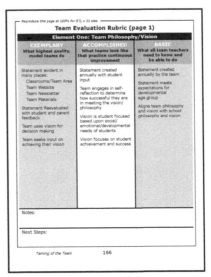

Full-page version on page 166

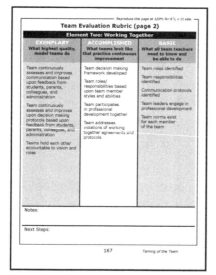

Full-page version
on page 167

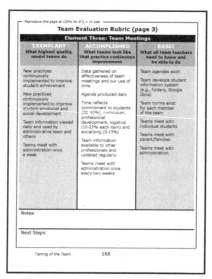

Full-page version
on page 168

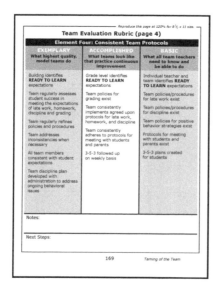

Full-page version
on page 169

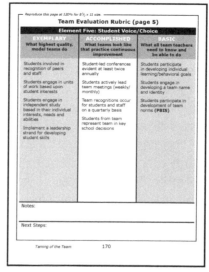

Full-page version
on page 170

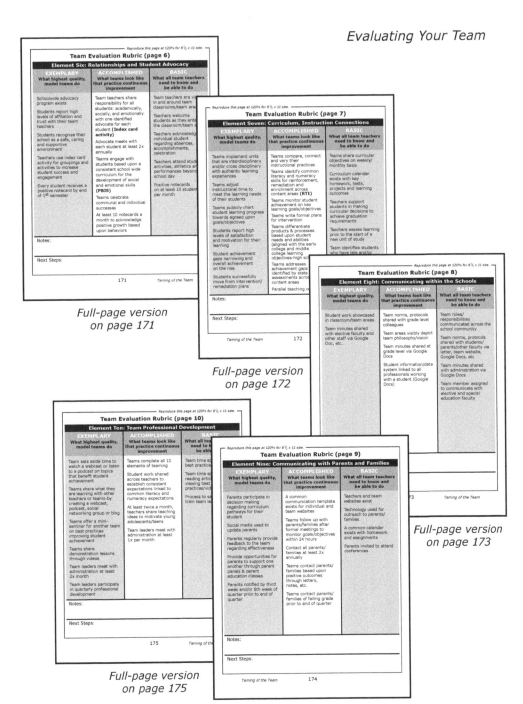

Reproduce this page at 120% for 8½ x 11 size.

Team Evaluation Rubric (page 6)
Element Six: Relationships and Student Advocacy

EXEMPLARY What highest quality, model teams do	ACCOMPLISHED What teams look like that practice continuous improvement	BASIC What all team teachers need to know and be able to do
Schoolwide advocacy program exists	Team teachers share responsibility for all students: academically, socially, and emotionally with one identified advocate for each student (**Index card activity**)	Team teachers are visible in and around team classrooms/team areas
Students report high levels of affiliation and trust with their team teachers		Teachers welcome students as they enter the classroom/team area
Students recognize their school as a safe, caring and supportive environment	Advocate meets with each student at least 2x annually	Teachers acknowledge individual student regarding absences, accomplishments, celebration
Teachers use index card activity for groupings and activities to increase student success and engagement	Teams engage with students based upon a consistent school wide curriculum for the development of social and emotional skills (**PBIS**)	Teachers attend student activities, athletics and performances beyond school day
Every student receives a positive notecard by end of 1st semester	Teams celebrate communal and individual successes	Positive notecards on at least 10 students per month
	At least 10 notecards a month to acknowledge positive growth based upon behaviors	

Notes:

Next Steps:

171   *Taming of the Team*

Full-page version on page 171

Reproduce this page at 120% for 8½ x 11 size.

Team Evaluation Rubric (page 7)
Element Seven: Curriculum, Instruction Connections

EXEMPLARY What highest quality, model teams do	ACCOMPLISHED What teams look like that practice continuous improvement	BASIC What all team teachers need to know and be able to do
Teams implement units that are interdisciplinary and/or cross disciplinary with authentic learning experiences	Teams compare, connect and vary their instructional practices	Teams share curricular objectives on weekly/ monthly basis
Teams adjust instructional time to meet the learning needs of their students	Teams identify common literacy and numeracy skills for reinforcement, remediation and enrichment across content areas (**RTI**)	Curriculum calendar exists with key homework, tests, projects and learning outcomes
Teams publicly chart student learning progress towards agreed upon goals/objectives	Teams monitor student achievement on key learning goals/objectives	Teachers support students in making curricular decisions to achieve graduation requirements
Students report high levels of satisfaction and motivation for their learning	Teams write formal plans for intervention	Teachers assess learning prior to the start of a new unit of study
Student achievement gaps narrowing and overall achievement on the rise	Teams differentiate products & processes based upon student needs and abilities (aligned with the early college and middle college learning objectives-high sch...	Team identifies students who have late and/or...
Students successfully move from intervention/ remediation plans	Teams addresses achievement gaps identified by state assessments acros... content areas	
	Parallel teaching o...	

Notes:

Next Steps:

Taming of the Team   172

Full-page version on page 172

Reproduce this page at 120% for 8½ x 11 size.

Team Evaluation Rubric (page 8)
Element Eight: Communicating within the Schools

EXEMPLARY What highest quality, model teams do	ACCOMPLISHED What teams look like that practice continuous improvement	BASIC What all team teachers need to know and be able to do
Student work showcased in classroom/team areas	Team norms, protocols shared with grade level colleagues	Team roles/ responsibilities communicated across the school community
Team minutes shared with elective faculty and other staff via Google Doc, etc.	Team areas visibly depict team philosophy/vision	Team norms, protocols shared with students/ parents/other faculty via letter, team website, Google Docs, etc
	Team minutes shared at grade level via Google Docs	Team minutes shared with administration via Google Docs
	Student information/data system linked to all professionals working with a student (Google Docs)	Team member assigned to communicate with elective and special education faculty

Reproduce this page at 120% for 8½ x 11 size.

Team Evaluation Rubric (page 10)
Element Ten: Team Professional Development

EXEMPLARY What highest quality, model teams do	ACCOMPLISHED What teams look like that practice continuous improvement	BASIC What all tea... need to k... be able...
Team sets aside time to watch a webcast or listen to a podcast on topics that benefit student achievement	Teams complete all 10 elements of teaming	Team time sp... best practice...
Teams share what they are learning with other teachers or teams-by creating a webcast, podcast, social networking group or blog	Student work shared across teachers to establish consistent expectations linked to common literacy and numeracy expectations	Team time sp... reading artic... viewing best practices/vid...
Teams offer a mini-seminar for another team on best practices improving student achievement	At least twice a month, teachers share teaching ideas to motivate young adolescents/teens	Process to se... train team le...
Teams share demonstration lessons through videos	Team leaders meet with administration at least 1x per month	
Team leaders meet with administration at least 2x month		
Team leaders participate in quarterly professional development		

Notes:

Next Steps:

175   *Taming of th...*

Full-page version on page 175

73   *Taming of the Team*

Full-page version on page 173

Reproduce this page at 120% for 8½ x 11 size.

Team Evaluation Rubric (page 9)
Element Nine: Communicating with Parents and Families

EXEMPLARY What highest quality, model teams do	ACCOMPLISHED What teams look like that practice continuous improvement	BASIC What all team teachers need to know and be able to do
Parents participate in decision making regarding curriculum pathways for their student	A common communication template exists for individual and team websites	Teachers and team websites exist
Social media used to update parents	Teams follow up with parents/families after formal meetings to monitor goals/objectives within 24 hours	Technology used for outreach to parents/ families
Parents regularly provide feedback to the team regarding effectiveness	Contact all parents/ families at least 2x annually	A common calendar exists with homework and assignments
Provide opportunities for parents to support one another through parent panels & parent education classes	Teams contact parents/ families based upon positive outcomes through letters, notes, etc.	Parents invited to attend conferences
Parents notified by third week and/or 6th week of quarter prior to end of quarter	Teams contact parents/ families of failing grade prior to end of quarter	

Notes:

Next Steps:

Taming of the Team   174

Full-page version on page 174

Rubric created by Annette Fante and Jack Berckemeyer.

Berckemeyer's Beliefs

Of course, you've heard plenty of my beliefs so far. You've read my whole philosophy about what makes teams work effectively for the big cause of improving life and learning for students.

But here are a few more things I vigorously believe to be true about teaming:

1. Team time is a gift—it is expensive for schools and school districts. Some school districts might decide that it would be easier to abandon teaming. It would mean fewer teachers and allow for teachers to teach one more class. However, if that happens, achievement will not increase, teacher morale will decline, and students will fall through the cracks. Actually, effective teaming saves time. Time wasters—such as lack of communication, lack of curriculum connection, multiple and confusing (and often conflicting) procedures and expectations, interventions needed because kids fell through the cracks or had no adult advocate—are avoided.

2. If we lose teaming in our schools, it will be because we did not effectively use our team time. As long as we continue to use the time to vent and complain, we will never see students succeed, and we will continue to ignore the natural connections in curriculum.

3. Sometimes, to be great, we have to drive through "Uglyville" and that means being frank with each other and not always worrying about hurting people's feelings. We need to hold each other accountable. High expectations are critical for students, but they are mandatory for us as teachers.

4. Team meetings are not about grading papers or cutting out stars for the display case.

5. Great teams sit together at a table—not in opposite areas of the room.

6. Taming the team is hard when educators are not committed to the teaming process. You may be a great teacher but work poorly with colleagues. If this is true of you, and if you have no commitment or motivation to work with others, teaming may not be for you. Try to land yourself in a situation where you do not work with a team. But I surely hope you try out a stint with a good team before you give up on it!

7. Teams who focus on kids, curriculum, and professional development increase student achievement, lower student referrals, and improve school climate.

8. Teams that offer enhancements and enrichment along with remediation see achievement increase for all students.

9. Teaming is hard, and dealing with adults is not easy.

10. Eating makes a meeting. When things get rough, bring in brownies.

11. Great administrators and counselors attend team meetings every two weeks.

12. Team leaders are really leaders! They are not evaluators!

13. Kids who have assigned adult advocates experience more success.

14. Teams divide up tasks. They don't focus on the one team member who will not work!

15. Teams hold kids in a class until the work is done—this is a great strategy for the student who can do the work, but chooses not to.

16. Teams treat parents with respect and thank them for being good parents and for trying. Team members sit next to parents, they never leave them alone. Teams offer them water or coffee, and tissues are always available.

Great teams embrace their inner lions! All of us who see the benefits to our students and ourselves that flow from effective teaming prize the model of good education. We are nourished by the growth of achievement, the healthy and productive climate for students, and the professionally supportive environment for ourselves. We defend the teaming concept. We know it works. We stand up and *roar* to promote it and keep it!

My Personal Experience with Teams

Working with a team is not always easy. It is often hard to put personal feelings aside. It is hard to confront colleagues, but it has to be done.

Maureen Rosekelly
7th Grade Intervention Specialist
Perkins Middle School

During my teaching career I have worked on two-, three-, and four-person teams. I have also worked with schools that have as many as 10 to 15 members on a team. The size of the team is not an issue. What counts is how effective they are when they meet.

I have loved and respected most of my teammates. There was one bad year that I tend to just block out and try to forget about, but that is life. It is not always perfect. In my career, I have tried to work well and play nice with others. Yet at times, I am sure I was frustrated and moody. I know for a fact that I might have pouted a couple of times when I did not get my way. But in the end, it was my teammates who kept me laughing, kept me on task, and made me a better teacher.

I am sure you noticed that I mentioned one team situation that might not have been the most positive experience of my life. To protect the innocent, I will not mention names or the school. However, sometime when I write my tell-all book about my life and my time in rehab (just kidding), I will mention specifics, dates and situations. So watch out for *Behind the Educational Curtain—The Life and Gossip of Jack Berckemeyer.*

In my years as a teacher, I worked with some great principals, like Mark Whitney, who really understood that teaming made his life easier. He understood that if teachers worked effectively together, they would be happier and healthier. He also knew when to rope teachers in, and when to let them soar. He was a lion tamer! Without him, I would never really have experienced the true meaning of teaming.

Mr. Whitney would hold team leader meetings once a month and would provide training for the team leaders. He would allocate funds to be used by the teams, and he held teachers accountable for the use of team time. He did not stand in the way. He allowed teams to lead.

> *School leaders are vital to the support of teaming. Even if they come from a high school or elementary level, they should know about the characteristics of middle level students and effective middle level teams!*
>
> *Annette Fante*
> *Former Assistant School Superintendent*
> *Douglas County Schools, Douglas County, Colorado*

Over the years, my teammates were all gifted and unique in their own way. I like to mention them so they can have the credit they deserve:

> I started off my teaching career working with Ms. Tossava, Mrs. Trumbo, and Mr. Gasman (Love that man and his name!). Later in my career, I worked with Ms. Martin, Mrs. Brakel, and Ms. Blatchford. All played a key role in my education as a teacher.

I can remember many occasions when my teammates would just look at me and shake their heads. It is true, I can be a Chihuahua on amphetamines. I also remember my teams laughing. I am sure we spent too much time discussing how one unique student might have set fire to his notebook in science class or how one of us might have said something silly in class.

The best stories always involved how middle school kids would use bodily functions during class to make everyone laugh. Those were good times, arguing over which kid could belch or pass gas like a pro. Good times!

But all in all, we worked together and remained focused on students. We got through the tasks and we took risks. At times we really did open the lion's mouth and insert our heads. Actually, we did bob for apples in a dirty horse bucket during one unit on the Olympics.

As a team, we met daily and never graded our papers or skipped a team meeting. Not unless we all were truly overwhelmed. We took risks, created interdisciplinary units, and really used flexible scheduling. We focused on our kids. We spent time meeting with our students and had endless meetings with parents. We changed around students' schedules, we moved our classes around, and we found ways to break out kids into smaller groups. It was wild and at times frustrating, but at the end of the year we would find time to celebrate at a local establishment and just laugh. Okay, we may have had one adult beverage that we all shared.

One thing I did learn early on about teaming is that you end up knowing more about your teammates than you need to know. No one needs to talk about or share a story about a rash. Repeat, no one needs to share about a rash! I guess it is true that during the school year you spend more time with your teammates than your significant other. I am sure that is why at times we pondered divorce from each other. We knew killing each other was not an option, because we all believed that we were too pretty for prison. Even during the tough times, it was nice to know that daily we would be meeting with at least one semimature adult. Though I know that is debatable.

I am thankful for my teams, and I am grateful to the teams that I have been working with for several years like Lima West, in Lima,

Ohio; Perkins Local School District, in Sandusky, Ohio; City of East Chicago School, in East Chicago, Indiana; Stillwater Middle School, in Stillwater, Oklahoma; Memorial Middle School and Whittier Middle school in Sioux Falls, South Dakota; Sandusky Middle and High schools in Sandusky, Ohio; and Arcola Intermediate, in Methacton School District, Eagleview, Pennsylvania.

It has been a pleasure watching these teams grow and prosper. They have come a long way, thanks to their team leaders, administration teams, and a marginal consultant who has pestered them for years. Yes, that's me!

During my teaching career, several teammates left the team and I was sad and even heartbroken. It is not a joyous occasion when someone we work with and we care about leaves to take another job or retires. We go through a sense of loss and may even become distraught over the idea of losing a teammate.

However, sometimes a teammate leaves the team and you hear your fellow teammates singing, "Ding, dong, the witch is . . . ." I know we experience some conflicts with team members. We have all wanted to pack up a noncooperative teammate's stuff. Being on a team leads to many emotions—some good and some not so good!

I have had many teachers tell me they started teaming with reservations. After all, we have people in the middle school who have been in a self-contained elementary classroom or teachers who have spent time working with only science teachers in a departmentalized setting. It can be difficult to work with others when you just want to close your door and teach. But teaching today is not about closing your door and doing your own thing. It is about collaboration and seeking new ways to deal with young adolescents. Some of the best teachers do not bury their heads in the sand. They spend time getting dirty and bobbing for apples in the big tank of school.

Discussion Guide

These questions will help guide the discussion of this book. Spend time as a team, school, or in your own solitude reflecting on your answers.

1. Have teams changed over the last 20 years?

2. What obstacles occur today that were concerns when teaming was first introduced?

3. What are your personal regrets and achievements regarding teaming?

4. If you have been on a team for a number of years, what have you learned along the way? If you are new to teaming, what are your worries or apprehensions?

5. Why is it so difficult to discuss an issue or concern during a team meeting?

6. In your career, what has been a highlight of your team time?

7. How has your team helped you in the last several years?

8. Is teaming worth fighting for, or has it run its course?

9. If you were asked to define teaming in 10 words, what words would you choose?

10. In your building, is teaming widely accepted, or just another passing fad?

11. Why is it so hard to work with adults?

12. What makes teaming easy?

13. After reading this book, what three things need to change right away regarding your team?

14. During the last year, did you or your team members use your team time to the best of your abilities?

15. If you were to tell a friend or a new teacher about the attributes of teaming, what would you tell her or him?

16. Have you ever been downright frustrated during a team meeting? What was the situation?

17. How should teachers handle conflict within the team?

18. Where do you see teaming heading in the next five years?

19. If you could ask the author one question, what would it be?

20. How difficult is it for teachers to stay on task during a team meeting?

21. Are you willing to make changes to how you approach team meetings?

22. How can you add a little more laughter to your team meetings?

23. Finally, did you learn at least one new idea regarding teaming from this book?

Taming of the Team

Additional Resources

This We Believe: Keys to Educating Young Adolescents (2010) organizes the 16 research-based characteristics of effective middle grades education into three areas:
- Curriculum, Instruction, and Assessment;
- Leadership and Organization; and
- Culture and Community.

In order to really implement the middle level concept, middle level educators must be willing to spend time as teams exploring these attributes.

An education for young adolescents must be

- **Developmentally responsive**

  Using the distinctive nature of young adolescents as the foundation upon which all decisions about school organization, policies, curriculum, instruction, and assessment are made.

- **Challenging**

  Ensuring that every student learns and every member of the learning community is held to high expectations.

- **Empowering**

  Providing all students with the knowledge and skills they need to take responsibility for their lives, to address life's challenges, to function successfully at all levels of society, and to be creators of knowledge.

- **Equitable**

  Advocating for and ensuring every student's right to learn and providing appropriately challenging and relevant learning opportunities for every student.

Characteristics of Successful Middle Level Schools
Curriculum, Instruction, and Assessment

- **Educators value young adolescents and are prepared to teach them.**
  Effective middle grades educators make a conscious choice to work with young adolescents and advocate for them. They understand the developmental uniqueness of this age group, the appropriate curriculum, effective learning and assessment strategies, and their importance as models.

- **Students and teachers are engaged in active, purposeful learning.**
  Instructional practices place students at the center of the learning process. As they develop the ability to hypothesize, to organize information into useful and meaningful constructs, and to grasp long-term cause and effect relationships, students are ready and able to play a major role in their own learning and education.

- **Curriculum is challenging, exploratory, integrative, and relevant.**
  Curriculum embraces every planned aspect of a school's educational program. An effective middle level curriculum is distinguished by learning activities that appeal to young adolescents, is exploratory and challenging, and incorporates student-generated questions and concerns.

- **Educators use multiple learning and teaching approaches.**
  Teaching and learning approaches should accommodate the diverse skills, abilities, and prior knowledge of young adolescents, cultivate multiple intelligences, draw upon students' individual learning styles, and utilize digital tools. When learning experiences capitalize on students' cultural, experiential, and personal backgrounds, new concepts are built on knowledge students already possess.

- **Varied and ongoing assessments advance learning as well as measure it.**
  Continuous, authentic, and appropriate assessment measures, including both formative and summative ones, provide evidence about every student's learning progress. Such information helps students, teachers, and family members select immediate learning goals and plan further education.

Leadership and Organization

- **A shared vision developed by all stakeholders guides every decision.**
  When a shared vision and mission statement become operational, middle level educators pursue appropriate practices in developing a challenging academic program; they develop criteria to guide decisions and a process to make needed changes.

- **Leaders are committed to and knowledgeable about this age group, educational research, and best practices.**
  Courageous, collaborative middle level leaders understand young adolescents, the society in which they live, and the theory of middle level education. Such leaders understand the nuances of teaming, student advocacy, exploration, and assessment as components of a larger middle level program.

- **Leaders demonstrate courage and collaboration.**
  Leaders understand that successful schools committed to the long-term implementation of the middle school concept must be collaborative enterprises. The principal, working collaboratively with a leadership team, focuses on building a learning community that involves all teachers and places top priority on the education and healthy development of every student, teacher, and staff member.

- **Ongoing professional development reflects best educational practices.**
  Professional development is a continuing activity in middle level schools where teachers take advantage of every opportunity to work with colleagues to improve the learning experiences for their students.

- **Organizational structures foster purposeful learning and meaningful relationships.**
  The ways schools organize teachers and group and schedule students have a significant impact on the learning environment. Interdisciplinary teams' common planning time, block scheduling, and elimination of tracking are related conditions that contribute to improved achievement.

Culture and Community

- **The school environment is inviting, safe, inclusive, and supportive of all.**
  A successful school for young adolescents is an inviting, supportive, and safe place, a joyful community that promotes in-depth learning and enhances students' physical and emotional well-being.

- **Every student's academic and personal development is guided by an adult advocate.**
  Academic success and personal growth increase markedly when young adolescents' affective needs are met. Each student must have one adult to support that student's academic and personal development.

- **Comprehensive guidance and support services meet the needs of young adolescents.**
  Both teachers and specialized professionals are readily available to offer the assistance many students need in negotiating their lives in and out of school.

- **Health and wellness are supported in curricula, school-wide programs, and related policies.**
  Abundant opportunities are available for students to develop and maintain healthy minds and bodies and to understand their personal growth through health-related programs, policies, and curricula.

- **The school actively involves families in the education of their children.**
  Schools and families must work together to provide the best possible learning for every young adolescent. Schools take the initiative in involving and educating families.

- **The school includes community and business partners.**
  Genuine community involvement is a fundamental component of successful schools for young adolescents. Such schools seek appropriate partnerships with businesses, social service agencies, and other organizations whose purposes are consistent with the school's mission.

I encourage teams to reference Incentive Publications Teaming Curriculum. This impactful 10-element training really forces teams to make radical changes toward effective use of team time. The curriculum focuses on kids, curriculum, and professional development. The program also provides quality professional development follow-up for the teams.

Elements of Effective Teaming

▶ Curriculum Overview
Day One: All-Staff Workshop
Day Two: Leadership Training

Ten Element Curriculum

Element 1 ▶Team Philosophy
Create a team philosophy; Achievement connection

Element 2 ▶Working Together as a Team
Roles and responsibilities of team members; Group decision-making;
Team self-reflection on how well the team works; Achievement connection

Element 3 ▶Effective Team Meetings
Norms and expectations for team meetings; Agendas for team meetings;
Good use of team time; Achievement connection

Element 4 ▶Consistent Team Protocols
Consistency items and processes; Team discipline policy;
Achievement connection

Element 5 ▶Student Voice and Choice
Rate current practices for voice and choice; Student surveys to elicit student
voice; Building team unity and identity; Connection to achievement

Element 6 ▶Building Relationships with Students
Advocacy groups; How to build relationships; Awards and celebrations;
Achievement connection

Element 7 ▶Curriculum-Instruction Connections
Curriculum connections; Instruction connections; Calendar connections;
Achievement connection

Element 8 ▶Communicating within the School
Evaluate current processes; Improve current processes;
Improve teacher-parent meetings and conferences; Achievement connection

Element 9 ▶Partnerships with Parents and Families
Evaluate current processes; Improve current processes;
Improve teacher-parent meetings and conferences; Achievement connection

Element 10 ▶Team Professional Development
A team professional development experience (model);
Planning for team professional development; Achievement connection

Thumbs Up, Thumbs Down

A Strategy for Developing Connections with Every Student

Many times we forget about certain students. The students that get most of our attention are the ones who need constant attention or those who are misbehaving. Yet, there are tons of students that are never mentioned during a team meeting.

During the "Thumbs Up, Thumbs Down" activity, the team will go over the entire team roster, mentioning each student. The team then picks a topic such as *missing work* or *students with three late assignments*. They give a thumbs up to any student who is not a concern regarding the topic. If they give a thumbs down, it means the student needs to have an intervention or some kind of support. In this way, a team can literally take a team roster of 120 and narrow the list down to about 30 who need help.

The team can then figure out strategies for how to help and support the student. For example, a teacher might keep the student in class for the entire day to finish work, or have the student go to the support center for some tutoring. Remember, nowhere is it written that you cannot hold a student after class to finish work. Just make sure you talk to the other teachers prior to holding the student in class.

Quick Research Overview

Research Points

▶ When teaming is effective, students do better academically, socially, and emotionally.

▶ Consistency in teaming, and in particular, plenty of common planning time, are positively related to increases in student achievement.

▶ Caring, trusting personal relationships between teachers and students lead to increases in student achievement. The stronger and more consistent such relationships, the greater the gains in student performance. Teaming supports such relationships between teachers and students.

▶ Students learn best in environments that are physically and emotionally safe and orderly. Teaming contributes greatly to such an environment.

▶ In settings where students have personalized, trusting relationships with adults, incidences of bullying are reduced, and students build stronger resilience to being bullied.

▶ The level of academic achievement that students attain by eighth grade has a larger impact on their college and career readiness by the time they graduate from high school than anything that happens academically in high school.

Taming of the Team

Questionnaire 1   DO NOT PUT YOUR NAME ON THIS.

GETTING TO KNOW YOUR TEAMMATES

Complete this questionnaire about yourself. Circle all of the choices that apply. You will be sharing your responses with your team. Find the response closest to reality that seems to fit you.

1. My favorite cuisine is
   A. Italian
   B. sugar-based
   C. meat and potatoes
   D. school lunch

2. On my iPod I do NOT have the following
   A. Barry Manilow
   B. Adele
   C. Respighi
   D. I don't own one.

3. The car I drive is
   A. really cool
   B. a hybrid
   C. in the shop a lot
   D. an unmarked car

4. If I weren't a teacher, I would be
   A. a rodeo clown
   B. a travel agent
   C. a therapist
   D. in therapy

5. For fun, I
   A. engage in athletic things, like running, volleyball, weightlifting
   B. read
   C. I don't do fun! Fun is the devil's playground.
   D. yell at kids

6. One of my favorite TV shows was/is
   A. L.A. Ink
   B. American Idol
   C. Hoarders
   D. The Colbert Report

7. My family thinks I am
   A. in witness protection
   B. totally cool
   C. a whiner
   D. a wiener

8. I wish my family thought I was
   A. in witness protection
   B. totally cool
   C. too fragile to have to work
   D. needier than I let on

9. When I relax, I like to wear
   A. P.J.s
   B. as little as possible
   C. sweats
   D. a cowboy outfit

10. I work best with others when
    A. they pretend to be cheerful
    B. they do as I say
    C. they leave me alone
    D. they bring food to the meetings

I think this survey belongs to _____.
signed _____

I think this survey belongs to _____.
signed _____

I think this survey belongs to _____.
signed _____

I think this survey belongs to _____.
signed _____

I think this survey belongs to _____.
signed _____

Questionnaire 2

Do You Really Know Your Teammates ?

As you think about them, answer the following.

Which of your teammates is most likely to:

1. Run, play volleyball, etc. in his or her spare time?_____

2. Drive a sports car if s/he could afford it? _____

3. Enjoy dressing up to go out?_____

4. Travel to exotic places for vacation?_____

5. Be in the Witness Protection Program?_____

6. Call his or her mom every day?_____

7. Moonlight?_____

8. Wear big fuzzy slippers at home?_____

9. Watch a reality show on TV?_____

10. Be writing a novel in his or her free time?_____

11. Own a circular saw?_____

12. Plan to visit Branson, MO, someday?_____

13. Have Susan Boyle on his or her iPod?_____

14. Keep band-aids/antiseptic in his or her car?_____

15. Hate sports?_____

16. Live to be 100?_____

17. Enjoy a Monster Truck show?_____

18. Eat more sugar than protein?_____

19. Sleep less than six hours each night?_____

20. Hate this survey?_____

Where Are We?

Team Expectations	Need to create	Need to discuss	Need to review	Completed
Is there a written team vision or mission?				
Are team roles and expectations established?				
Are team roles suited to each team member?				
Is there a set team meeting agenda?				
Has the team set consistent policies and procedures?				
Is curriculum discussed during team meetings?				
Has the team set a name?				
Does the team celebrate communal events and successes (for students and teachers)?				
Is homework for the week discussed by the team?				
Is a team calendar created and referenced?				
Does the team have a student information log?				
Can team members identify student workloads for the week?				

Where Are We? page 2

Team Expectations	Need to create	Need to discuss	Need to review	Completed
Does the team follow up on tasks by assigning roles and responsibilities?				
Is there a set team grading policy?				
Is there a parent contact sheet? Does the team discuss parent issues and concerns?				
Are there established norms for team meetings?				
Are outside resources used (counselor or administrators)?				
Does the team share new teaching strategies and ideas?				
Does the team read or study books together?				
Does the team spend time evaluating student work?				
Is there a process for team communication with support staff?				
Does the team regularly discuss ways to integrate curriculum? (How often?)				
How many days a week does the team meet?				
Does the team discuss strategies for advisory, flex class, or homeroom?				

Taming of the Team

Sample Philosophy-Vision Statements

Team Unity
—
Our Vision Statement

1 **We believe:** that our students need a supportive environment; that the development of a sense of belonging and commitment is crucial to our success as a community of learners.
Therefore: In order to grow and learn together, our entire community of students and teachers will agree to live by certain values and expectations.
Team Unity's core values are the Distinctions of Integrity, which are: respect, responsibility, communication, commitment, honesty, trust, participation, and collaboration.

2 **We believe:** that our young adolescent students need opportunities for exploration.
Therefore: Much of the learning on this team will occur in exploratory settings with students making discoveries for themselves. Project-based learning is a cornerstone of our philosophy of good education.

3 **We believe:** that students grow when they interact with others; that they learn from one another in significant ways.
Therefore: We will create many opportunities for students to work with partners and small groups.

4 **We believe:** that, as teachers, we are here to guide students while helping them acquire the skills and understandings necessary to move forward in school and in life.
Therefore: Students will be responsible for their learning and for communicating their progress with parents through student-led conferences.

Incentive Publications, Teaming Curriculum

We Stand For This . . .

We care about all of our kids.

To show this . . .

. . .*we will listen to and respect each one.*

. . .*we will assign one adult to each student to assure that he or she has a personal advocate.*

. . .*we will discuss our students every week to best meet their needs.*

Fireballs
Sheridan
Middle School

We believe young adolescents need to take responsibility for themselves and their learning.

To show this . . .
we will give students real responsibilities and chances for decision-making.

We believe young adolescents learn best through exciting, engaging learning experiences.

To show this . . .

. . . we will deal with important, relevant ideas in our curriculum.

. . . we will structure activities that get kids discussing, moving, planning, and creating.

We believe that cooperative teaching leads to deeper understandings of concepts.

To show this . . .
. . . we will plan interdisciplinary units.
. . . we will cooperate in planning instructional strategies.

Incentive Publications, Teaming Curriculum

Taming of the Team

Team Philosophy-Vision
Dolphin Team, 2010-2011

Our team is committed to the academic success
of each student, and we will do what it takes
to see that each one achieves.

To that end, during the 2010-2011 academic year, we will:

1. Ascertain each student's current academic level
   in each subject we teach.

2. Work with others, including parents, former teachers,
   and current staff to devise stategies specific
   to each child for his or her success.

3. Work thoughtfully with each student to set goals
   and understand his or her learning style.

4. Work daily to monitor progress and regroup and rethink
   when necessary.

5. Call in outside sources immediately when the need arises.

Evaluation:

1. Mastery of materials

2. A significant (25% or better) reduction
   in behavioral incidents

3. Greater (80% or better) student participation
   in team activities

4. Overall academic growth of 10-20%

5. Few (less than 5%) absentees

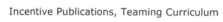

Incentive Publications, Teaming Curriculum

Some Decision-Making Models

▶ **Plus and Minus Overview**
Make a plus and minus column for each possible decision. List the
pros (reasons why this is a good solution) and cons (reasons why this
might not be a good solution). When the list is finished,
make the choice that has the most compelling list of *pros*.

▶ **Flow Chart**
Identify the decision to be made. Identify two
or more possible choices. Then use a visual diagram
to show what events, actions, consequences, or other
issues would result from each choice.

▶ **Multi-Voting**
Each member votes on as many solutions as she or he likes.
The solution that gets the most votes is the team decision.

▶ **Multi-Voting With A Twist**
Each member has five votes that he or she can divide
among alternate decisions in any configuration. The
solution that gets the most votes is the team decision.

▶ **Chart The Components**
Analyze the issue and create possible outcomes to view
and evaluate. First, define the issue. Then list possible
decisions. For each decision, detail what the action would
look like and what the consequences would be.
(See Support Piece 2-I for an example.)

▶ **What We Can Live With**
Each member lists what she or he can live with.
The team chooses a decision that is on everybody's list.

▶ **Cause And Effect Chain**
Consider varying possible decisions by writing them
as "If...Then..." statements. This shows the results
and consequences that are likely to flow from
different decisions. Team members review the list
of statements to see which decision has the
greatest number of agreeable "Then" statements.

▶ **Majority Rules**
Take a straight-out vote! Follow the
viewpoint of the majority and move on.

Incentive Publications, Teaming Curriculum

Taming of the Team

Seaside Team 7-A   **Team Meeting Agenda**

Team _____ Date _____

Members Present _____

_____

Past business:

_____

_____

_____

_____

_____

Today's business:

Emergency concerns

Action Items		
Decision-Action	Person(s) Responsible	Timeline

Sample Agenda 2

Meeting Agenda and Documentation

Explorers
Team

Date _____ **Members Present Initials**

_____ _____ _____ _____ _____

time	**Item**	**Decision**
_____ 1.		
_____ 2.		
_____ 3.		
_____ 4.		
_____ 5.		
_____ 6.		

Next Steps   *Who*   *When?*

1.

2.

3.

4.

Items for Next Agenda

Taming of the Team

Sample Agenda 3

Grizzly Team Meeting Agenda

Members Present

Old Business Follow-Up:

New Discussion:

Time	Item to Discuss	Decision	Follow-Up Who and When?
	1		
	2		
	3		
	4		
	5		
	6		

Emergency Items and Logistics

Time	Item to Discuss	Decision	Follow-Up Who and When?
	1		
	2		
	3		
	4		

Discipline Process Form

Issue

Response

Examples

Response

Proactive Interventions

Response

Strategies

Response

Responses and Documentation

Response

Taming of the Team

Graphic Resources

Response

Response

Response

Response

Response

Discipline Process Form *page 2*

Consequences and Rewards

Follow-up

Support

Last Resort Idea

Administrative Decision

Taming of the Team

3-5-3 PLANNING FORM

Student name _____ Date _____

(3) Issues: _____

    1.

    2.

    3.

(5) Strategies for moving forward

    1.

    2.

    3.

    4.

    5.

(3) Ways to follow up

    1.

    2.

    3.

Student signature _____

Parent or guardian signature _____

Teacher signature _____

Taming of the Team

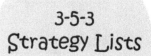

3-5-3
Strategy Lists

Classroom Teacher-initiated Intervention

▶ Conference with student
▶ Signed agenda
▶ Phone conference with parent
▶ Daily progress report notification of grades and progress
▶ Use of peer tutor
▶ Simplified assignments
▶ Provide scribe notes for student
▶ Have student repeat directions
▶ Weekly assistance with organization
▶ Provide help at lunch or after school
▶ Verbal checks for understanding
▶ Use of advanced organizers
▶ Plan of improvement
▶ Adult mentor
▶ Class recommendations
▶ Team study hall recommendations
▶ Student strategies
▶ Records homework assignments in agenda
▶ Asks for help when necessary
▶ Attends help sessions, lunch, before/after school
▶ Organizes binder weekly
▶ Uses daily progress report or signed agenda

Student Services Involvement

▶ Weekly progress report
▶ Academic contract
▶ Care and concern process initiated
▶ Reduce or break-up assignments
▶ Pacing instructions (slower/faster)
▶ Offer alternative assessment
▶ Modify tests/assignments
▶ Simplified reading assignments
▶ ADD or ADHD referral
▶ Child study meeting
▶ Discussion at team meeting re: academics
▶ Conference with parent, student, counselor, administrator, mental health representatives, teachers

Parental Involvement

▶ Tutoring or alternative learning settings considered
▶ Follow up on academic contract

3-5-3 Follow-up Ideas

▶ Student returns to team meeting in a week to make sure there has been some progress. This is critical and should be added to all 3-5-3 interventions.

▶ Call the parent.

▶ Notify the counselor.

▶ Create a self-monitoring check list for the student.

▶ Use of agenda book—check and verify that the agenda book is being completed.

▶ Notify principal.

▶ Add 3-5-3 to student folder.

▶ Seek student input after a couple weeks of activating the 3-5-3 plan.

Taming of the Team

LOOKING AT ALL THE ELEMENTS THAT AFFECT STUDENTS

CONSIDER ALL OF THESE AREAS WHEN CREATING A 3-5-3.

Social Issues
Questions to consider

- How does the student relate to peers?

- Is the student able to work in a group?

- Is the student mature for his/her age or lacking in basic social skills?

- Is there another student who works well with this student?

- Are there rewards that allow the student to spend time with friends?

Emotional Issues
Questions to consider

- How does the student react to praise or when corrected for bad behaviors?

- Is the student quick to anger or passive aggressive?

- Is the student prone to cry or emotional out-bursts?

- Does the student need praise and constant support?

- What methods get the student to respond in a positive manner?

Academic Issues
Questions to consider

- What information can you gather from the student's past test scores?

- Areas of concern in academics?

- Specific skills in which the student has not shown proficiency?

- Grades and missing work issues?

Outside Influences
Questions to consider

- Does the student have support at home?

- Has the student had issues that affect his/her work at school?

- Is the student able to do homework in a safe and secure environment?

- Do parents follow through on plans and teacher ideas?

- Are there medications or abuse issues?

- Is counseling or any support provided to the student or family?

- Recent death in family or family health issues?

- Currently dealing with divorce?

LOOKING AT ALL THE ELEMENTS THAT AFFECT STUDENTS

CONSIDER ALL OF THESE AREAS WHEN CREATING A 3-5-3.

Outside Influences
Questions to consider

Academic Issues
1s to consider

Emotional Issues

Social Issues
Questions to consir-

Taming of the Team

Our Connection **Goals**

Curriculum Connections for Week of _____
(dates)

Teacher name:_____ Subject: _____

Connection	Did You Do It?	How Did It Work?
1.		
2.		
3.		

Teacher name:_____ Subject: _____

Connection	Did You Do It?	How Did It Work?
1.		
2.		
3.		

Teacher name:_____ Subject: _____

Connection	Did You Do It?	How Did It Work?
1.		
2.		
3.		

Teacher name:_____ Subject: _____

Connection	Did You Do It?	How Did It Work?
1.		
2.		
3.		

Team _____ Date _____

Instructional Connections for Week of _____

Teacher name:_____ Subject: _____

Instructional Practice to Use	For Lesson on	How Did It Work?
1.		
2.		
3.		

Teacher name:_____ Subject: _____

Instructional Practice to Use	For Lesson on	How Did It Work?
1.		
2.		
3.		

Teacher name:_____ Subject: _____

Instructional Practice to Use	For Lesson on	How Did It Work?
1.		
2.		
3.		

Teacher name:_____ Subject: _____

Instructional Practice to Use	For Lesson on	How Did It Work?
1.		
2.		
3.		

Team _____ Date _____

Taming of the Team

Graphic Resources

Calendar
Connections   for Week of _____

▶ **Here's what we learned from looking**
at our calendar for next week:

▶**Here are the adjustments we made:**

▶**We commit to these general principles and practices:**

▶**Here's when we will follow up to evaluate these commitments:**

Team _____ Date _____

Incentive Publications, Teaming Curriculum

Taming of the Team   160

Ways to Connect ▶ Curriculum

In order to connect curriculum, teams must have a comprehensive understanding of the course of study in each core area. This requires ongoing conversation and sharing. Curriculum mapping is important and can be undertaken to any degree by a team—even if the whole school isn't involved.

You can't make curriculum connections effectively without (intentionally) wandering into other kinds of connections, such as in instruction, scheduling, and assessment. In planning to connect curriculum across the team—to any extent—think beyond just the topics or ideas you will connect. Think about many facets that are a part of "doing" your curriculum across the team, and try to standardize approaches and expectations for those also:

- What you will study (specific topics)
- What big understandings or concepts you hope students to acquire
- Specific skills students will need to use and improve
- How the information, processes, and experiences will be delivered
- How the learning process will be assessed along the way
- What kinds of evidence students will produce to show what they learn
- How you will assess a final product or set of understandings

Look for connections in content—starting with the obvious chances for topical integration (for example, students study the Civil War in social studies while language arts classes read a novel set in that time period; science study of weather is supported by math classes working on scale models of hot air balloons or calculating volume of gas in weather balloons). But focus more time on looking for connections in concepts and themes that are relevant and critical across subject areas. Examples ▶

- **change**
- **risk**
- **movement**
- **patterns and systems**
- **cycles**
- **rules**
- **structure**
- **order and organization**
- **conflict**
- **authority**
- **boundaries**
- **resistance to change**
- **scarcity**
- **resources**
- **transitions**
- **causes and effects**

Incentive Publications, Teaming Curriculum

Taming of the Team

Find skills and processes that are needed across the disciplines.
Agree on common formats and expectations for students to create, learn,
or use these. Coordinate your schedules to use the skills during the same
time period. Examples:

- **note-taking**   • **critical reading**   • **critical thinking**
- **essay-writing**   • **vocabulary mastery**   • **summarizing**
- **using portfolios**   • **reflecting**   • **reading maps, charts, graphs**

Work together to help students master standards. Over a period of
several weeks, commit to addressing standards. Take one chunk of your
grade-level standards at a time, and use some planning time to see how
the knowledge or skills involved can be strengthened by the whole team.

**Establish a testing calendar and various processes to support
students.** This might mean that
- the team simply agrees to not give tests on the same day.
- the team flexes the schedule to allow all students to take a *big* test first
  thing in the morning and then adjusts the day's schedule accordingly.
- no other teacher assigns a heavy project due that same day.
- when a big test is approaching, the teacher creates a study guide and
  shares it across the team. Other teachers may use it in some way
  that practices a skill their students need anyway.

Start small. Ease into integration with manageable connections:
- Try a two-subject integration built around a common subject or theme
  (such as language arts and social studies focus on the American
  Revolution, Civil War or another era in history).
- Try a two-subject integration built around a common process (such as
  science and math work on problem-solving steps OR social studies and
  science practice of steps for investigations).
- Try a two, three, or four-subject integration of a single lesson around
  a common theme such as patterns or verification.
- Try an all-subject integration for practicing a skill such as summarization.

Incentive Publications, Teaming Curriculum

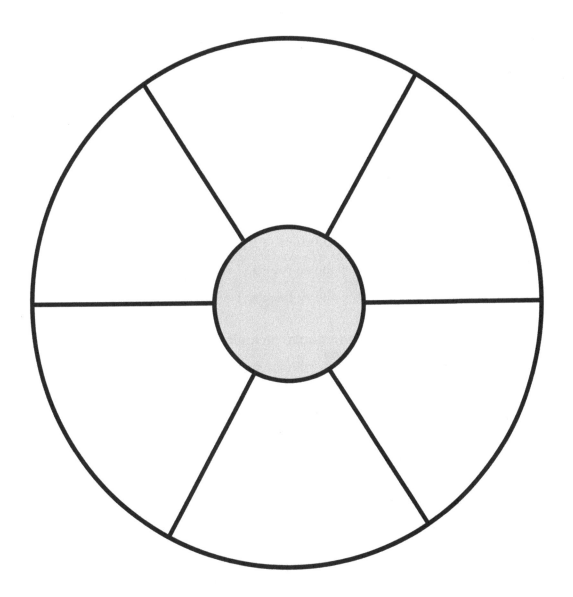

Taming of the Team

Team Reflection

Circle the response that most accurately describes your team.

1 **Our team meets**
At least 3 times a week
At least 3 times a month
At least 3 times a semester
It at least meets.

2 **When we refer to students on our team, we**
Call them by name
Call them names
Use "what's his name"
Use nicknames ("Mr. Bigmouth." "Ms. Goth Beauty")

3 **For professional development (PD), our team**
Sends a team member to a conference every few years
Has a regular day scheduled for PD
Reads an article once
Thinks "PD" meant "Puberty Development" and refers it to the counselor

4 **Our team has common goals, including**
Getting through the year
Getting through the year without hurting each other
Getting through to the students
Making specific plans for student success

5 **Our team regularly looks at data in order to**
Seem smarter than we are
Please the administration
Help us with Sudoku
Work together to strategize areas where students need help

6 **When teams collaborate regarding curriculum and instruction**
Everything gets garbled
Kids get time off
Kids make better academic connections
Teachers take turns teaching

7 **Our team communicates with our students' families by**
Website
Oversight
Eyesight
Blindsides

8 **Teams allow students to have a choice in their own learning because**
Students are more motivated
Teachers have less to do
Teachers don't know as much as kids
Kids today are more independent

9 **When my team meeting is scheduled to begin**
I am in my seat eating the first piece of cake
I arrive fashionably late
I am ready with required materials
I am busy elsewhere

10 **I like working on a team because**
I have less to do
I like the food at the meetings
I know it's great for kids
I am basically a sad, lonely person

11 **Our team communicates with other teams in our school/grade**
When they do something we don't like
Whenever we distribute our team minutes so everyone knows what's up
Whenever we want to suck up to the administration
Whenever we challenge them to a rumble in the faculty lounge

12 **When it comes to disciplining students on our team**
We rely on the principal
We rely on our common discipline policy
We rely on the guillotine
We rely on prayer

13 **An example of common policies and procedures on our team is**
We don't allow anything
No shirt, no shoes, no sit at desk
We have common requirements for late work
We are not late to work

14 **We share responsibilities on our team by**
Taking turns bringing food
Taking turns sharing the meeting and preparing the agenda
Taking turns as lookout in case the principal comes
Taking turns badmouthing the students

15 **As part of our teaming effort, we celebrate with our students**
Especially on their days off
Especially when we are tired
Especially when they have success
Especially when a parent sends brownies

Team Evaluation Rubric (page 1)

Element One: Team Philosophy/Vision

EXEMPLARY What highest quality, model teams do	ACCOMPLISHED What teams look like that practice continuous improvement	BASIC What all team teachers need to know and be able to do

Statement evident in many places:
    Classrooms/Team Area
    Team Website
    Team Newsletter
    Team Materials
 	
Statement reevaluated with student and parent feedback
 	
Team uses vision for decision making
 	
Team seeks input on achieving their vision
	Statement created annually with student input
	
	Team engages in self-reflection to determine how successful they are in meeting the vision/philosophy
	
	Vision is student focused based upon social/emotional/developmental needs of students
	
	Vision focuses on student achievement and success
		Statement created annually by the team
		
		Statement meets expectations for developmental age group
		
		Aligns team philosophy and vision with school philosophy and vision

Notes:

Next Steps:

Team Evaluation Rubric (page 2)

Element Two: Working Together

EXEMPLARY What highest quality, model teams do	ACCOMPLISHED What teams look like that practice continuous improvement	BASIC What all team teachers need to know and be able to do
Team continuously assesses and improves communication based upon feedback from students, parents, colleagues, and administration Team continuously assesses and improves upon decision-making protocols based upon feedback from students, parents, colleagues, and administration Teams hold each other accountable to vision and roles	Team decision-making framework developed Team roles/ responsibilities based upon team member styles and abilities Team participates in professional development together Team addresses violations of working together agreements and protocols	Team roles identified Team responsibilities identified Communication protocols identified Team leaders engage in professional development Team norms exist for each member of the team

Notes:

Next Steps:

Taming of the Team

Team Evaluation Rubric (page 3)

Element Three: Team Meetings

EXEMPLARY What highest quality, model teams do	ACCOMPLISHED What teams look like that practice continuous improvement	BASIC What all team teachers need to know and be able to do
New practices continuously implemented to improve student achievement	Data gathered on effectiveness of team meetings and use of time	Team agendas exist
New practices continuously implemented to improve student emotional and social development	Agenda produced daily	Team develops student information system (e.g., folders, Google Docs™)
Team information viewed daily and used by administrative team and others	Time reflects commitment to students (30-40%), curriculum, professional development, logistics (10-25% each item) and socializing (5-15%)	Team norms exist for each member of the team
Teams meet with administration once a week	Team information available to other professionals and updated regularly	Teams meet with individual students
	Teams meet with administration once every two weeks	Teams meet with parent/families
		Teams meet with administration

Notes:

Next Steps:

Team Evaluation Rubric (page 4)

Element Four: Consistent Team Protocols

EXEMPLARY What highest quality, model teams do	ACCOMPLISHED What teams look like that practice continuous improvement	BASIC What all team teachers need to know and be able to do
Building identifies **READY TO LEARN** expectations Team regularly assesses student success in meeting the expectations of late work, homework, discipline, and grading Team regularly refines policies and procedures Team addresses inconsistencies when necessary All team members consistent with student expectations Team discipline plan developed with administration to address ongoing behavioral issues	Grade level identifies **READY TO LEARN** expectations Team policies for grading exist Team consistently implements agreed upon protocols for late work, homework, and discipline Team consistently adheres to protocols for meeting with students and parents 3-5-3 followed up on weekly basis	Individual teacher and team identifies **READY TO LEARN** expectations Team policies/procedures for late work exist Team policies/procedures for discipline exist Team policies for positive behavior strategies exist Protocols for meeting with students and parents exist 3-5-3 plans created for students

Notes:

Next Steps:

Taming of the Team

Team Evaluation Rubric (page 5)

Element Five: Student Voice/Choice

EXEMPLARY What highest quality, model teams do	ACCOMPLISHED What teams look like that practice continuous improvement	BASIC What all team teachers need to know and be able to do
Students involved in recognition of peers and staff	Student-led conferences evident at least twice annually	Students participate in developing individual learning/behavioral goals
Students engage in units of work based upon student interests	Students actively lead team meetings (weekly/ monthly)	Students engage in developing a team name and identity
Students engage in independent study based in their individual interests, needs, and abilities	Team recognitions occur for students and staff on a quarterly basis	Students participate in development of team norms (PBIS)
Implement a leadership strand for developing student skills	Students from team represent team in key school decisions	

Notes:

Next Steps:

Team Evaluation Rubric (page 6)

Element Six: Relationships and Student Advocacy

EXEMPLARY	ACCOMPLISHED	BASIC
What highest quality, model teams do	What teams look like that practice continuous improvement	What all team teachers need to know and be able to do
Schoolwide advocacy program exists Students report high levels of affiliation and trust with their team teachers Students recognize their school as a safe, caring and supportive environment Teachers use index card activity for groupings and activities to increase student success and engagement Every student receives a positive notecard by end of 1st semester	Team teachers share responsibility for all students: academically, socially, and emotionally with one identified advocate for each student (Index card activity) Advocate meets with each student at least 2x annually Teams engage with students based upon a consistent schoolwide curriculum for the development of social and emotional skills (PBIS) Teams celebrate communal and individual successes At least 10 notecards a month to acknowledge positive growth based upon behaviors	Team teachers are visible in and around team classrooms/team area Teachers welcome students as they enter the classroom/team area Teachers acknowledge individual student regarding absences, accomplishments, celebration Teachers attend student activities, athletics, and performances beyond the school day Positive notecards on at least 10 students per month

Notes:

Next Steps:

Taming of the Team

Team Evaluation Rubric (page 7)

Element Seven: Curriculum, Instruction Connections

EXEMPLARY	ACCOMPLISHED	BASIC
What highest quality, model teams do	**What teams look like that practice continuous improvement**	**What all team teachers need to know and be able to do**
Teams implement units that are interdisciplinary and/or cross disciplinary with authentic learning experiences	Teams compare, connect and vary their instructional practices	Teams share curricular objectives on weekly/ monthly basis
Teams adjust instructional time to meet the learning needs of their students	Teams identify common literacy and numeracy skills for reinforcement, remediation, and enrichment across content areas	Curriculum calendar exists with key homework, tests, projects, and learning outcomes
Teams publicly chart student learning progress toward agreed upon goals/objectives	Teams monitor student achievement on key learning goals/objectives	Teachers support students in making curricular decisions to achieve graduation requirements
Students report high levels of satisfaction and motivation for their learning	Teams write formal plans for intervention	Teachers assess learning prior to the start of a new unit of study
Student achievement gaps narrowing and overall achievement on the rise	Teams differentiate products and processes based upon student needs and abilities (aligned with the early college and middle college learning objectives—high school)	Team identifies students who have late and/or missing work
Students successfully move from intervention/ remediation plans	Teams address achievement gaps identified by state assessments across content areas	
	Parallel teaching occurs	

Notes:

Next Steps:

Team Evaluation Rubric (page 8)

Element Eight: Communicating within the Schools

EXEMPLARY What highest quality, model teams do	ACCOMPLISHED What teams look like that practice continuous improvement	BASIC What all team teachers need to know and be able to do
Student work showcased in classroom/team areas Team minutes shared with elective faculty and other staff via Google Docs™, etc.	Team norms, protocols shared with grade-level colleagues Team areas visibly depict team philosophy/vision Team minutes shared at grade level via Google Docs™ Student information/data system linked to all professionals working with a student (Google Docs™)	Team roles/ responsibilities communicated across the school community Team norms, protocols shared with students/ parents/other faculty via letter, team website, Google Docs™, etc. Team minutes shared with administration via Google Docs™ Team member assigned to communicate with elective and special education faculty

Notes:

Next Steps:

Taming of the Team

Team Evaluation Rubric (page 9)

Element Nine: Communicating with Parents and Families

EXEMPLARY What highest quality, model teams do	ACCOMPLISHED What teams look like that practice continuous improvement	BASIC What all team teachers need to know and be able to do
Parents participate in decision making regarding curriculum pathways for their student Social media used to update parents Parents regularly provide feedback to the team regarding effectiveness Provide opportunities for parents to support one another through parent panels and parent education classes Parents notified by third week and/or sixth week of quarter prior to end of quarter	A common communication template exists for individual and team websites Teams follow up with parents/families after formal meetings to monitor goals/objectives within 24 hours Contact all parents/families at least twice a year Teams contact parents/families based upon positive outcomes through letters, notes, etc. Teams contact parents/families of failing grade prior to end of quarter	Teachers and team websites exist Technology used for outreach to parents/families A common calendar exists with homework and assignments Parents invited to attend conferences

Notes:

Next Steps:

Team Evaluation Rubric (page 10)

Element 10: Team Professional Development

EXEMPLARY What highest quality, model teams do	ACCOMPLISHED What teams look like that practice continuous improvement	BASIC What all team teachers need to know and be able to do
Team sets aside time to watch a webcast or listen to a podcast on topics that benefit student achievement	Teams complete all 10 elements of teaming	Team time spent sharing best practices
Teams share what they are learning with other teachers or teams by creating a webcast, podcast, social networking group or blog	Student work shared across teachers to establish consistent expectations linked to common literacy and numeracy expectations	Team time spent sharing/ reading articles and/or viewing best instructional practices/videos
Teams offer a mini-seminar for another team on best practices improving student achievement	At least twice a month, teachers share teaching ideas to motivate young adolescents/teens	Process to select and train team leaders
Teams share demonstration lessons through videos	Team leaders meet with administration at least once a month	
Team leaders meet with administration at least twice a month		
Team leaders participate in quarterly professional development		

Notes:

Next Steps:

Taming of the Team

About the Author

A nationally recognized presenter, author, and humorist, Jack Berckemeyer began his career as a middle school teacher in Denver, Colorado. After two years of teaching, he was named as an outstanding educator at his school, and shortly thereafter he was identified as one of the outstanding educators in the district. In 2003, he received the Outstanding Alumni Award from the Falcon School District.

Jack is known for communicating a message of hope, laughter, and insight into the nature of the young adolescent. He served for 13 years as the Assistant Executive Director for the National Middle School Association, now Association for Middle Level Education (AMLE), and is the author of *Managing the Madness: A Practical Guide to Middle Grades Classrooms* and co-author of the professional development curriculum, *The Elements of Effective Teaming.*

Jack is currently the Director for Nuts & Bolts Symposiums for Middle Level Educators held in Destin, Florida, and Boulder, Colorado.

In 2012, Jack was awarded the Paul George Award from the Florida League of Middle Schools and the James Garvin Award from the New England League of Middle Schools. The Ohio Middle Level Association previously selected Jack as their Outstanding Educator.

Jack lives in Denver, Colorado, and has no pets or plants.